OPPOSING
VIEWPOINTS®
SERIES

Gateway Drugs

Other Books of Related Interest:

Opposing Viewpoints Series

Alcohol

Teen Drug Abuse

At Issue Series

Alcohol Abuse

Should the Legal Drinking Age Be Lowered?

Teen Smoking

"Congress shall make no law . . . abridging the freedom of speech, or of the press."

First Amendment to the U.S. Constitution

The basic foundation of our democracy is the First Amendment guarantee of freedom of expression. The *Opposing Viewpoints* Series is dedicated to the concept of this basic freedom and the idea that it is more important to practice it than to enshrine it.

Gateway Drugs

Noël Merino, Book Editor

GREENHAVEN PRESS
A part of Gale, Cengage Learning

Detroit • New York • San Francisco • New Haven, Conn • Waterville, Maine • London

Christine Nasso, *Publisher*
Elizabeth Des Chenes, *Managing Editor*

© 2008 Greenhaven Press, a part of Gale, Cengage Learning

Gale and Greenhaven Press are registered trademarks used herein under license.

For more information, contact:
Greenhaven Press
27500 Drake Rd.
Farmington Hills, MI 48331-3535
Or you can visit our Internet site at gale.cengage.com

Articles in Greenhaven Press anthologies are often edited for length to meet page requirements. In addition, original titles of these works are changed to clearly present the main thesis and to explicitly indicate the author's opinion. Every effort is made to ensure that Greenhaven Press accurately reflects the original intent of the authors. Every effort has been made to trace the owners of copyrighted material.

Cover photograph © 2008/Jupiterimages

LIBRARY OF CONGRESS CATALOGING-IN-PUBLICATION DATA

Gateway drugs / Noël Merino, book editor.
    p. cm. -- (Opposing viewpoints)
  Includes bibliographical references and index.
  ISBN-13: 978-0-7377-4002-8 (hardcover)
  ISBN-13: 978-0-7377-4003-5 (pbk.)
  1. Drug abuse. I. Merino, Noël.
  HV5809.5.G38 2008
  362.29--dc22
                                                    2008008134

Printed in the United States of America
1 2 3 4 5 6 7 12 11 10 09 08

Contents

Chapter 3: What Is the Relationship Between Gateway Drugs and Other Drugs?

Chapter 4: What Should Society Do About Gateway Drugs?

Why Consider Opposing Viewpoints?

> *"The only way in which a human being can make some approach to knowing the whole of a subject is by hearing what can be said about it by persons of every variety of opinion and studying all modes in which it can be looked at by every character of mind. No wise man ever acquired his wisdom in any mode but this."*
>
> *John Stuart Mill*

In our media-intensive culture it is not difficult to find differing opinions. Thousands of newspapers and magazines and dozens of radio and television talk shows resound with differing points of view. The difficulty lies in deciding which opinion to agree with and which "experts" seem the most credible. The more inundated we become with differing opinions and claims, the more essential it is to hone critical reading and thinking skills to evaluate these ideas. Opposing Viewpoints books address this problem directly by presenting stimulating debates that can be used to enhance and teach these skills. The varied opinions contained in each book examine many different aspects of a single issue. While examining these conveniently edited opposing views, readers can develop critical thinking skills such as the ability to compare and contrast authors' credibility, facts, argumentation styles, use of persuasive techniques, and other stylistic tools. In short, the Opposing Viewpoints Series is an ideal way to attain the higher-level thinking and reading skills so essential in a culture of diverse and contradictory opinions.

In addition to providing a tool for critical thinking, Opposing Viewpoints books challenge readers to question their own strongly held opinions and assumptions. Most people form their opinions on the basis of upbringing, peer pressure, and personal, cultural, or professional bias. By reading carefully balanced opposing views, readers must directly confront new ideas as well as the opinions of those with whom they disagree. This is not to simplistically argue that everyone who reads opposing views will—or should—change his or her opinion. Instead, the series enhances readers' understanding of their own views by encouraging confrontation with opposing ideas. Careful examination of others' views can lead to the readers' understanding of the logical inconsistencies in their own opinions, perspective on why they hold an opinion, and the consideration of the possibility that their opinion requires further evaluation.

Evaluating Other Opinions

To ensure that this type of examination occurs, Opposing Viewpoints books present all types of opinions. Prominent spokespeople on different sides of each issue as well as well-known professionals from many disciplines challenge the reader. An additional goal of the series is to provide a forum for other, less known, or even unpopular viewpoints. The opinion of an ordinary person who has had to make the decision to cut off life support from a terminally ill relative, for example, may be just as valuable and provide just as much insight as a medical ethicist's professional opinion. The editors have two additional purposes in including these less known views. One, the editors encourage readers to respect others' opinions—even when not enhanced by professional credibility. It is only by reading or listening to and objectively evaluating others' ideas that one can determine whether they are worthy of consideration. Two, the inclusion of such viewpoints encourages the important critical thinking skill of objectively evaluating an author's credentials and bias. This evaluation will illuminate an author's reasons for taking a particular stance on an issue and will aid in readers' evaluation of the author's ideas.

It is our hope that these books will give readers a deeper understanding of the issues debated and an appreciation of the complexity of even seemingly simple issues when good and honest people disagree. This awareness is particularly important in a democratic society such as ours in which people enter into public debate to determine the common good. Those with whom one disagrees should not be regarded as enemies but rather as people whose views deserve careful examination and may shed light on one's own.

Thomas Jefferson once said that "difference of opinion leads to inquiry, and inquiry to truth." Jefferson, a broadly educated man, argued that "if a nation expects to be ignorant and free . . . it expects what never was and never will be." As individuals and as a nation, it is imperative that we consider the opinions of others and examine them with skill and discernment. The Opposing Viewpoints Series is intended to help readers achieve this goal.

David L. Bender and Bruno Leone,
Founders

Introduction

> *"There is a false perception that if a drug is legal it must cause less problems. In many countries and cultures, the use of alcohol and/or tobacco is so deeply woven into the cultural fabric of those countries that neither is acknowledged as a drug or even as a problem."*—*Drug Watch International, May 15, 2001*

According to Merriam-Webster's Dictionary, a drug is "a substance other than food intended to affect the structure or function of the body." Under this definition, the following all are considered drugs: legal pharmaceutical drugs; legal over-the-counter drugs; legal drugs such as nicotine and alcohol; illegal drugs such as marijuana, cocaine, methamphetamine, and heroin. All of the mentioned drugs above are regulated, to some extent, by the U.S. government by different policies.

Whereas pharmaceutical drugs are only available by prescription, over-the-counter drugs such as cold medicines are available in drugstores, though are regulated by the Food and Drug Administration (FDA). Nicotine in tobacco products is available to people over the age of eighteen (nineteen in Alabama, Alaska, and Utah) in the form of cigarettes, cigars, and chewing tobacco. Alcohol is available to people over the age of twenty-one, with different state laws across the country regulating availability and public consumption of different types of alcohol. Marijuana, cocaine, methamphetamine, and heroin (among other drugs) are illegal in the United States (with about a dozen states allowing personal possession for medical use). The different policies that regulate the availability and use of these drugs have their root in varying justifications and are widely debated.

The usage of different drugs correlates somewhat to the legal status. According to data in 2006 from the U.S. Department of Health and Human Services' Substance Abuse and Mental Health Services Administration (SAMHSA), 45.4 percent of persons twelve and older have used illicit drugs: whereas 39.8 percent have used marijuana, only 14.3 have used cocaine and 1.5 percent have used heroin. The percentages of use are much higher for legal substances: as of 2006, among persons twelve and older, 70.7 percent had used tobacco products and 82.7 percent had used alcohol.

Many debates about drug policies, including the issue of legal status, focus on assessing the dangers of the drug in question. One kind of danger to consider is the direct harm to the user caused by the use of the drug itself. For example, the Drug Enforcement Administration (DEA) says that use of methamphetamine "can cause mental confusion, severe anxiety, and paranoia." These types of harms have caused many to argue that methamphetamine is appropriately illegal. Similarly, on the topic of cocaine use, the National Institute on Drug Abuse (NIDA) notes, "Regardless of how cocaine is used or how frequently, a user can experience acute cardiovascular or cerebrovascular emergencies, such as a heart attack or stroke, which can result in sudden death." On the other hand, a perceived lack of danger is what has caused many to argue that marijuana ought to be legal. The Drug Policy Alliance claims, "Over the past century, numerous reports from independent, government-sponsored commissions have documented the drug's [marijuana's] relative harmlessness and recommend the elimination of criminal sanctions for consumption-related offenses." Direct dangers to the user, however, are not the only kinds of dangers considered when evaluating drug policy.

The gateway theory of drug use, popular since the 1980s, provides an additional factor to consider when evaluating the dangers of drugs. According to the theory, the use of certain drugs such as tobacco, alcohol, and marijuana makes the user more likely to use more dangerous drugs such as cocaine and heroin. If this theory is true, then this danger needs to also be evaluated when considering the appropriate social policies for a given drug. The drugs most commonly referred to as gateway drugs are alcohol, tobacco, and marijuana. Whereas alcohol and tobacco are legal, though regulated, marijuana is illegal. In determining whether the current policies, including legal status, are appropriate, the gateway claims need to be evaluated. For instance, while the relative immediate harms of alcohol and tobacco may provide a basis for distinguishing them from drugs like cocaine and methamphetamine, if the gateway theory is accurate, there may be reason to reconsider the milder policies toward such substances.

In *Opposing Viewpoints: Gateway Drugs*, authors debate current issues about gateway drugs in the following chapters: Do Certain Drugs Have a Gateway Effect? Are Gateway Drugs Harmful? What Is the Relationship Between Gateway Drugs and Other Drugs? What Should Society Do About Gateway Drugs? The many viewpoints included in this volume demonstrate that there is wide disagreement about the existence of gateway drugs, the dangerousness of said drugs, and the solutions to dealing with these substances that will continue to offer much opportunity for debate.

OPPOSING
VIEWPOINTS®
SERIES

CHAPTER 1

Do Certain Drugs Have a Gateway Effect?

Chapter Preface

The theory that certain drugs provide a gateway for use of other drugs is a theory that is not easy to prove or disprove. Certain data can appear to provide anecdotal evidence for the theory. For instance, Robert Hornik cites data correlating the use of alcohol and tobacco with the use of marijuana: "Whereas about 4% of those with no use of alcohol or cigarettes initiated marijuana use, 24% with one type of prior use and 44% of those who had previous experience with both alcohol and cigarettes initiated marijuana use in the subsequent 18 months." Correlation, however, is not the same as causation.

To prove causation, correlation is required but not sufficient. For example, statistics may show that 34 percent of people who eat pancakes later use marijuana—this statistic shows a correlation between eating pancakes and using marijuana. However, it would be a fallacy to infer causation from this correlation. Additional information supporting the existence of a causal relationship between pancake eating and marijuana use would need to be identified in order to support a causal relationship. This type of fallacy of inferring causation from a correlation is often referred to as *false cause* or, in Latin, *cum hoc ergo propter hoc* (with this, therefore because of this).

For a gateway effect to be established between certain drugs, causation needs to be established. Marijuana is one of the most common drugs to be identified as a gateway drug. Proponents of the theory claim that marijuana use provides a gateway for the use of other drugs such as cocaine and heroin. Often put forward in support of the view is the fact that many cocaine and heroin users used marijuana before using cocaine or heroin. But this correlation has an alternate explanation. The Institute of Medicine explains, "Because it is the most widely used illicit drug, marijuana is predictably the first illicit drug most people encounter. Not surprisingly, most users of other illicit drugs have used marijuana first." It is not surprising that, if one uses drugs of different sorts, that marijuana would be the first one people try because it is the most widely available. For any drug to be proven to be a gateway drug, the drug's effects must have a causal connection to further drug use.

Authors examine this issue further in the following chapter. Determining whether data about drug use shows that certain drugs are causally linked to the use of other drugs, or merely correlated, is a critical part of assessing whether these drugs have a gateway effect.

> *"Studies cast doubt on whether experimentation at one stage is necessary to use of substances associated with later stages."*

The Theory That Some Drugs Have a Gateway Effect Is Debatable

David J. Hanson

In the following viewpoint, David J. Hanson interviews Andrew L. Golub. Golub explains the gateway and stepping stone theories, both of which suggest that the use of certain "soft" drugs, like tobacco and alcohol, lead to the use of "hard" drugs. He claims that both theories are flawed. Golub cites studies that contradict these theories and explains how the theories can negatively affect public policy. Hanson is professor emeritus of sociology at the State University of New York, Potsdam. Golub received his PhD in public policy analysis from Carnegie Mellon University. He is currently a principal investigator at the National Development and Research Institute in New York City.

David J. Hanson, "Gateway and Steppingstone Substances: An Interview With Dr. Andrew L. Golub," *Alcohol: Problems and Solutions*, September 10, 2007. www2.potsdam.edu/hansondj/YouthIssues/1104198586.html. Reproduced by permission.

As you read, consider the following questions:

1. According to Andrew Golub, what is the stepping stone theory of drug progression?
2. How does Golub describe the gateway theory of drug progression?
3. Does Golub believe there is evidence for either the stepping stone theory or the gateway theory?

D*r. David J. Hanson: Dr. Golub, could you explain the similarities and differences between the popular Gateway and Stepping Stone theories?*

Dr. Andrew L. Golub: The idea that one behavior leads to another is an old one going back hundreds of years. The Stepping Stone and Gateway theories or metaphors each suggest something slightly different about the nature of substance use progression. There is a theory that youths typically start substance use with alcohol and tobacco which are widely used by adults but whose use is prohibited to youths. Some of these individuals progress to marijuana use and some marijuana users progress to hard drugs. The two different metaphors have different suggestions about the inevitability of the progression.

The Stepping Stone metaphor brings to mind stones leading across a stream. It suggests that once a person takes the first step, crossing the water to the other side is inevitable. Presumably the opposite bank represents hard drug use, hard drug abuse and all of the attendant consequences. Thus, a youth who has had a taste of alcohol or tobacco is destined to smoke marijuana, then go on to hard drugs such as cocaine, crack, heroin and LSD. Additionally, the individual is in grave danger of being swept downstream by the current representing the dangers of substance use progression unless the person returns to the original side, which metaphorically corresponds to non-substance use.

In contrast, the Gateway metaphor suggests a series of gates leading into successive pastures. A person can pass through one gate and spend time in the first field representing alcohol and tobacco use and perhaps never go through subsequent gates leading to marijuana and hard drug use. Passing through each gate exposes the individual to new risks.

Differences Between the Stepping Stone and Gateway Theories

So the Stepping Stone theory suggests that the progression to more dangerous substances is inevitable unless the user gives up all the substances (stepping stones) and returns to the safe side (abstinence), never to take even one step across the water?

You got it. By adopting this metaphor as if it were true, many policy advocates have strongly called for abstinence and zero tolerance of any youthful substance use. Indeed, the latest statement of the Nation's drug policy from the White House calls for zero tolerance of under age alcohol and tobacco use.

The Gateway theory seems to be less extreme than the Stepping Stone. It's obvious that using one substance doesn't inexorably result in hard drug use and abuse.

That's right. If you stick to a very literal interpretation of the two metaphors.

Could those who have entered the "hard drug use field" return to the "marijuana field," never to go back to hard drugs like cocaine?

Yes. In fact, the authors of the Monitoring the Future Study, a program which interviews high school seniors every year, have found that individuals cut back and even quit the use of various substances toward the end of young adulthood.

Evidence For the Theories

Are these theories supported by evidence from the real world?

At the superficial level, there is much evidence that individuals initiate alcohol and tobacco use at earlier ages than marijuana and hard drug use. However, the evidence is clearly inconsistent with the rigid progression implied by the Step-

The Difference Between the Stepping Stone and Gateway Hypotheses, Applied to Marijuana

The gateway analogy evokes two ideas that are often confused. The first, more often referred to as the "stepping stone" hypothesis, is the idea that progression from marijuana to other drugs arises from pharmacological properties of marijuana itself. The second is that marijuana serves as a gateway to the world of illegal drugs in which youths have greater opportunity and are under greater social pressure to try other illegal drugs. . . .

The stepping stone hypothesis applies to marijuana only in the broadest sense. People who enjoy the effects of marijuana are locally, logically, more likely to be willing to try other mood-altering drugs than are people who are not willing to try marijuana or who dislike its effects. In other words, many of the factors associated with a willingness to use marijuana are, presumably, the same as those associated with a willingness to use other illicit drugs. Those factors include physiological reactions to the drug effect, which are consistent with the stepping stone hypotheses, but also psychological factors, which are independent of drug-specific effects. There is no evidence that marijuana serves as a stepping stone on the basis of its particular physiological effect. . . ..

Whereas the stepping stone hypothesis presumes a predominantly physiological component of drug progression, the gateway theory is a social theory. The latter does not suggest that the pharmacological qualities of marijuana make it a risk factor for progression to other drug use. Instead, the legal status of marijuana makes it a gateway drug.

Institute of Medicine, Marijuana and Medicine: Assessing the Science Base, *Washington, D.C. National Academy Press, 1999, p. 99.*

ping Stone metaphor. In fact, several recent studies even suggest a substantial proportion of those individuals who became hard drug users did not follow the gateway sequence. In 1994, I published the results of a study of substance use progression of mostly crack abusers from inner-city New York. It found that these individuals were just as likely to have started with marijuana use as alcohol use and that those individuals born in more recent years were even more likely to have started with marijuana use. Analyses of at least three other samples have also found that a substantial proportion of hard drug users had not followed the gateway sequence. These studies cast doubt on whether experimentation at one stage is necessary to use of substances associated with later stages.

Personally, my preferred metaphor is one that is widely used in the psychology literature, the markers metaphor. I suggest that use of alcohol, tobacco, and marijuana serve as "markers" of those youths who are at increased risk of hard drug use. The image here is that of a network of roadways. Along one path is the typical "gateway" sequence to hard drugs, but there are other paths leading to hard drugs. Most importantly, there are many paths involving adolescent substance use leading to otherwise fine outcomes in young adulthood.

So the popular idea that preventing people from using the first gateway substance is faulty because it wouldn't prevent them from using illegal drugs?

That's right.

Who Goes Through the Gateway

Does the Gateway theory tell us who will pass through one gateway and who won't?

There is much theory about psychological and sociological factors associated with increased risk of substance use and other factors which tend to protect individuals from such use.

However, it is important to note that the association here is statistical; progression is not automatic.

There are three central domains which affect an individual's reaction: the substance used, the person's mind set, and the social setting in which use occurs. All three of these factors are important and it is a gross oversimplification to suggest that use of one substance inexorably leads to another. The progression of which substances an individual uses clearly occurs within a cultural context and, importantly, an individual's progress is affected by their place in that culture as well as other personal factors.

Your approach seems to be realistic and based on the actual behavior of people, doesn't it?

Thank you.

Why the Theories are Popular

Given the obvious inadequacies of the Stepping Stone and Gateway theories, why are they so popular?

I suspect there are a variety of reasons. Graham Allison has indicated that there are three domains—rational, institutional and political—which affect the formation of public policy. The wealth of scientific findings inform the rational perspective. It is convenient to reduce this often dry stack of findings to a simple metaphor. Convenient, but not always correct. The gateway and stepping stone metaphors are particularly compelling because, if they were true, they provide a clear foundation for early substance abuse prevention, a problem of great concern. The true solution to this problem is probably much more complicated as are most problems regarding human behavior and our social condition.

From the institutional perspective, there are many agencies and policies dedicated to preventing adolescent substance use. Making important sounding statements based on the gateway theory provides a useful justification for larger budgets, increased staff, and job security.

From the political perspective, there are varied interest groups which appear to be increasingly intolerant of people taking individual risks. These groups are concerning themselves with a wide range of behaviors, automobile air bags, the use of child seats in cars, second-hand smoke, and adolescent substance use. Supporting a theory, like the gateway theory, helps propel their concerns to the forefront.

The Effectiveness of Zero Tolerance

You mentioned zero tolerance earlier. How effective is this approach to the problem?

I suspect that even if you could keep youths from using alcohol and tobacco, this would not reduce substance abuse. I say "could" because our nation has been engaging in a "war against drugs" for decades, use of alcohol and tobacco are prohibited for youths, yet most youths experiment with both before reaching the age of legal majority. So, I seriously question whether all youthful substance use could ever be prevented. Moreover, by energetically opposing all use we might actually be promoting abuse. You [David Hanson] have written extensively on the cultural theory of alcohol use. This theory suggests that learning how to drink from responsible members of the community is the best way to assure that individuals will incorporate alcohol use into a functional lifestyle, if they choose to use. Cross-cultural comparisons suggest that in groups that are intolerant of alcohol use, there are more individuals whose use has led to personal and social problems. I suspect that there is much merit to this theory.

You've studied this subject for many years. Based on your expertise, what public or eductional policy would you recommend to reduce substance abuse?

I am not happy with the increasing intolerance of youthful substance use. I feel that we are prematurely branding individuals as criminals as opposed to reaching out and trying to help them with their problems. On the other hand, I do not recommend any dramatic changes at this time, like lowering the drinking age. Dramatic social changes can be very disruptive and lead to unintended consequences. I would recommend a policy similar to what has prevailed in the last 30 years and that is grudging tolerance. This would result in an official policy which in effect says we do not condone your substance use; however, if you ever need help in thinking through your problems, we're here for you. Such a policy would allow educators and other professionals to work with youths and to help them in any way they possibly can. The way current policies are moving, a youth would need to pledge abstinence as a precondition to counseling or else risk criminal penalties.

> *"Once use of tobacco or alcohol begins,
> there is greater likelihood of marijuana
> use, and once marijuana use begins,
> there is greater likelihood of other ille-
> gal drug use."*

Some Drugs Have a Gateway Effect

Kimberly R. Martin

*In the following viewpoint, Kimberly R. Martin reports on new
research in favor of the theory that certain drugs have a gateway
effect. In particular, the research indicates that alcohol and tobacco are gateway drugs to marijuana, while marijuana is a
gateway drug to other illegal drugs, such as cocaine. The research
also identifies drug exposure opportunities as a significant factor
that contributes to illegal drug use. Kimberly R. Martin is a contributing writer for NIDA Notes, a publication of the U.S. government produced by the National Institute on Drug Abuse
(NIDA).*

Kimberly R. Martin, "Youths' Opportunities to Experiment Influence Later Use of Illegal Drugs," *NIDA Notes*, vol. 17, January 2003. www.drugabuse.gov/NIDA_notes.

As you read, consider the following questions:

1. According to the research, what percentage of alcohol and tobacco users reported an opportunity to try marijuana by the age of eighteen? What percentage of this group used marijuana?

2. What percentage of nonsmokers and nondrinkers does Martin cite as having reported an opportunity to try marijuana by the age of eighteen? What percentage of this group used marijuana?

3. In Martin's view, how can an understanding of the gateway theory help parents and doctors in their drug prevention efforts?

NIDA-supported [National Institute on Drug Abuse] researchers have reported new epidemiological evidence about the associations linking earlier alcohol or tobacco use with later use of marijuana, and the link from earlier marijuana use to later use of other illegal drugs such as cocaine and hallucinogens. This study builds on the many prior NIDA-supported studies of the "gateway" theory of youthful drug involvement: Once use of tobacco or alcohol begins, there is a greater likelihood of marijuana use, and once marijuana use begins, their is greater likelihood of other illegal drug use.

"This research increases our understanding of the complex relationship between the different stages of drug use and raises concerns about factors that promote the transition from opportunities to initiate drug use to patterned use," says Dr. Kathleen Etz of NIDA's Division of Epidemiology, Services and Prevention Research. "We know that earlier drug use is associated with later, more advanced use; however, this research identifies a previously overlooked aspect of this transition, opportunities to use."

The Gateways to Marijuana and Cocaine

Using annual data from the 1991 through 1994 National Household Survey on Drug Abuse (NHSDA), the research team, led by Dr. James C. Anthony from Johns Hopkin's University Bloomberg School of Public Health in Baltimore, analyzed the responses of 26,015 individuals aged 12 to 18 who answered questions regarding marijuana use and the responses of 44,624 individuals aged 12 to 25 who answered questions regarding cocaine use. The research focused on a concept called "drug exposure opportunities." This concept takes into account that some young people actively seek out opportunities to try marijuana or cocaine, whereas others are more passive recipients of drug exposure opportunities.

The researchers found that alcohol and tobacco users were more likely than nonusers to have an opportunity to try marijuana and were also more likely to try the drug when the opportunity arose. About 75 percent of alcohol or tobacco users reported an opportunity to try marijuana by age 18, and more than 85 percent of them made the transition to marijuana use. Only about 25 percent of nonsmokers and nondrinkers were given an opportunity to try marijuana by the same age. Of these, fewer than 25 percent began smoking marijuana within 6 years after they were first given the opportunity. Overall, alcohol or tobacco users were seven times more likely to start using marijuana than individuals who had used neither alcohol nor tobacco.

Prior marijuana use was closely associated with the opportunity to try cocaine and the likelihood of young people's starting to use cocaine once given the opportunity. Among the young people who were given the chance to try cocaine, those who were already using marijuana were 15 times more likely to use cocaine than those who did not use marijuana. About 50 percent of marijuana users used cocaine within 2 years of their first opportunity to do so. However, among young people who never used marijuana, fewer than 10 percent initiated cocaine use.

Evidence of a Gateway Effect

The results of this [2002] study add new epidemiologic evidence to an already abundant body of literature on a possibly causal association linking earlier use of alcohol and tobacco to later marijuana use, and on a separate association linking earlier use of marijuana to use of other illegal drugs such as cocaine. For many years, alcohol and tobacco use has been described as a "gateway" experience with respect to subsequent use of marijuana and other illegal drugs. Nevertheless, the "gateway" concept is merely descriptive and does not seek to explain mechanisms that might operate to link alcohol or tobacco use with later use of marijuana or to link marijuana use with use of cocaine. . . . The main observations of this study were: 1) use of a drug in one stage is associated with an increased likelihood of encountering an exposure opportunity to make the transition towards the next stage of involvement in illegal drug use; 2) prior use of one drug is associated with an increased likelihood of actually starting to use the next drug in the sequence, once an exposure opportunity has occurred; and 3) observed sequences from alcohol and tobacco use to marijuana and cocaine use cannot be explained solely by differential drug-seeking behavior once drug use has occurred, to the extent that we were able to constrain drug-seeking by requiring an appreciable lag time from first opportunity to first drug use.

F.A. Wagner and J.C. Anthony,
"Into the World of Illegal Drug Use:
Exposure Opportunity and other Mechanisms Linking
the Use of Alcohol, Tobacco, Marijuana, and Cocaine,"
American Journal of Epidemiology, 2002.

Drug Exposure Opportunities

In a separate but related study, the researchers analyzed data from 41,271 young people who participated in the 1991 through 1994 NHSDA, investigating the relationship between the use of marijuana and use of hallucinogens. The results showed that marijuana users are more likely than nonusers to be offered an opportunity to use LSD, mescaline, mixed stimulant-hallucinogens, and PCP and more likely than nonusers to try these hallucinogenic drugs when they're offered. By age 21, nearly one-half of the teenagers who had smoked marijuana were presented with the opportunity to try hallucinogens, compared to only only-sixteenth of those who had not used marijuana. Once given the opportunity to use hallucinogens, marijuana smokers were about 12 times more likely to use hallucinogens than those who did not use marijuana.

"These studies are the first to support the idea of two separate mechanisms linking the use of alcohol, tobacco, marijuana, cocaine, and hallucinogens—one mechanism involving increased drug exposure opportunity, and a separate mechanism involving increased likelihood to use once the opportunity occurs," says Dr. Anthony. "Even if there is an underlying common vulnerability or predisposition that accounts for the observed sequencing of drug exposure opportunities and actual drug use, these observations may have implications for the design and evaluation of drug prevention activities. Drug users often are members of social circles where drug use and experimentation are more common and friends are likely to share drugs. In addition to trying to persuade young people not to use drugs, it may be worthwhile for us to persuade users not to share their drugs with friends." Previous research has also shown that although males are more likely than females to have opportunities to use drugs, both are equally likely to make a transition into drug use once an opportunity to try a drug has occurred. Dr. Anthony and his colleague, Dr. Fernando Wagner, also from John Hopkins University Bloomberg School of Public Health, have made similar observations in ongoing research studies.

Illegal Drug Use Prevention

Dr. Anthony believes that his research carries a strong message for parents and pediatricians, who often neglect the opportunity ask children and adolescents about whether they have had chances to try illegal drugs. As Dr. Anthony notes, "Kids will talk to us about their chances to try illegal drugs even when they are unwilling to talk about actual drug use. Once the chance to try marijuana or cocaine occurs, it is a red flag, and we need to be paying close attention to what happens next."

"Future research in this area will be a great asset to the development of effective drug prevention programs," says Dr. Etz. "It will assist us in understanding the process through which the use of one drug is related to use of another and help us to target prevention programs to individuals more likely to progress to advanced substance use."

> "It may well be that most hard drug ad-
> dicts started off as soft drug users, but
> one cannot conclude from that fact that
> hard drug use is caused by previous ex-
> perience of soft drugs."

Little Evidence Exists of a Causal Gateway Effect

Stephen Pudney

In the following viewpoint, Stephen Pudney argues that there is very little evidence for the theory that using soft drugs (including tobacco, alcohol, and marijuana) causes the use of hard drugs (cocaine, crack, and heroin). Pudney suggests that an individual's use of drugs, soft or hard, may be the result of personal characteristics. Pudney concludes that harsh public policy on soft drugs may have the unintended consequence of making the correlation between soft drugs and hard drugs even stronger. Stephen Pudney is a professor at the University of Essex within the Institute for Social and Economic Research.

As you read, consider the following questions:

1. What alternative explanation does Pudney provide for why soft drug use usually precedes hard drug use?

Stephen Pudney, *The Road to Ruin? Sequences of Initiation into Drug Use and Offending by Young People in Britain*, London: Home Office Research, Development and Statistics Directorate, 2002. Copyright © 2002 Crown. Reproduced by permission.

2. What does Pudney suggest as a reason why people are prone to look at the data on drug use and assume that soft drugs have a gateway effect on use of hard drugs?

3. Within the survey data that Pudney analyzes, what kind of correlation is there between soft drug use, and use of crack and heroin?

This is a study of the occurrence and timing of young people's first use of various types of illicit drug and their first experience of various types of offending, including truancy. Its aim is to investigate the gateway effect—the hypothesis that use of soft drugs leads to a higher future risk of hard drug use and crime.

The Evidence for the Gateway Theory

The study makes use of information from the 1998/99 Youth Lifestyles Survey (YLS), which yields a set of around 3,900 interviews in which young people make a confidential report of their own experience of drug use and offending. They do this, unobserved by any other individual, by responding to questions generated automatically on the screen of a laptop computer.

On the surface, the YLS data seem broadly consistent with some variants of the gateway theory, in the sense that the age of onset for most soft drugs is less than the age of onset for most hard drugs. For example, the average age of first use of glue/solvents and cannabis are 14.1 and 16.6 years respectively, compared with 17.5 and 20.2 years for heroin and cocaine. However, there are anomalies: for example ecstasy has an average age of onset of 18.9 years compared to 17.5 years for heroin.

There is much less evidence of a gateway effect for drugs into crime. The average age of onset for truancy and crime are 13.8 and 14.5 years respectively, compared with 16.2 for drugs generally and 19.9 years for hard drugs. Thus crime tends to precede drug use rather than vice versa.

Statistically Significant "Gateway" Responses

Use of:	Correlation (of 95% or More) With Future Use of:					
	Tobacco	Alcohol	Marijuana	Cocaine	Crack	Heroin
Tobacco	N/A	+	+		+	
Alcohol	+	N/A	+	+		
Marijuana	+	+	N/A	+		

TAKEN FROM: Stephen Pudney, "The Road to Ruin? Sequences of Initiation Into Drug Use and Offending by Young People in Britain," Home Office Research, Development, and Statistics Directorate, December 2002.

These links are investigated at the individual level, allowing for the influence of gender, ethnicity, family background, location, age and the prevalence of drug 'culture' in society at large. Superficially, this more detailed analysis still suggests a pattern of responses roughly consistent with the gateway hypothesis.

An Alternative Explanation of the Data

However, this conclusion could be unreliable. Suppose, for example, that a difficult family and social background predisposes a young person towards 'antisocial' behaviour. Soft drugs and minor crime offer the easiest avenues for the very young to offend but opportunity widens with age. so we tend to find an association between early soft drug use and later hard drug use. But, in this example, the association is at least partly spurious. Early soft drug use and later hard drug use may be joint expressions of the same underlying personal problem rather than a consequence of a causal influence of soft drug use on the subsequent desire for harder drugs. The apparent progression from soft to hard drugs may be just a consequence of the fact that soft drugs are easier to get and more affordable than hard drugs for the very young.

There are statistical techniques available to isolate the role of unobservable factors (such as a social or psychological predisposition towards antisocial behaviour) and thus solve this problem of spurious association. These methods work by trying to infer each individual's underlying predisposition from his/her general tendency towards early or late onset.

Little Evidence of a Gateway Effect

After applying these methods, there is very little remaining evidence of any causal gateway effect. For example, even if soft/medium drugs (cannabis, amphetamines, LSD, magic mushrooms, amyl nitrite) could somehow be abolished completely, the true causal link with hard drugs (crack, heroin, methadone) is found to be very small. For the sort of reduction in soft drug use that might be achievable in practice, the predicted causal effect on the demand for hard drugs would be negligible. Although there is stronger evidence of a gateway between soft drugs and ecstasy/cocaine, it remains small for practical purposes.

My interpretation of the results of this study is that true gateway effects are probably very small and that the association between soft and hard drugs found in survey data is largely the result of our inability to observe all the personal characteristics underlying individual drug use.

It is dangerous to read too much into the empirical association between early soft drug use and subsequent hard drug use. It may well be that most hard drug addicts started out as soft drug users, but one cannot conclude from that fact that hard drug use is caused by previous experience of soft drugs. There may be many confounding social and psychological factors which are hard to observe and measure, and which simultaneously contribute to the drive towards both soft and hard drugs. Once an attempt is made to correct statistical estimates for the likely effects of these confounding factors, the implied gateway effects become much smaller.

What the Analysis Shows

The analysis, based on recent survey data on nearly 4,000 children and young adults, finds:

- No significant impact of soft drug use on the risk of later involvement with crack and heroin.

- Very little impact of soft drug use on the risk of later involvement in crime.

- A significant but small gateway effect probably exists linking soft drug use to the social drugs ecstasy and cocaine. However, after correcting for the likely effect of underlying unobservable factors, the predicted long-run consequence of even a complete removal of soft drugs from the scene would only be a one-third cut in the prevalence of ecstasy and cocaine.

The policy implications of gateway effects are not straightforward. Even if it is true that soft drug use increases the risk of later involvement in hard drugs and crime, this does not automatically justify the adoption of a strict policy on soft drugs. By linking soft and hard drugs under the same banner of illegality, a strict policy stance may have the perverse effect of amplifying the gateway effect and increasing the prevalence of hard drugs in the long run. Before translating empirical findings on the size of gateway effects into policy prescriptions, one must have a clear idea of how the gateway effect arises.

In any case, gateway effects are probably too small to be a major factor in the design of anti-drug policy. Other approaches, such as education, treatment and various types of local initiative, are more likely to be effective than a general campaign against soft drugs.

Social, economic and family circumstances seem to be the dominant influences on young people's risk of becoming involved in crime and drug use. Indirect policies, aimed at problems of local deprivation and family breakdown may offer at least as much hope as more direct anti-drug and anti-crime policies.

"Although marijuana gateway effects may truly exist, available evidence does not favor the marijuana gateway effect over the alternative hypothesis."

The Evidence for a Gateway Effect Is Inconclusive

Andrew R. Morral, Daniel F. McCaffrey, and Susan M. Paddock

In the following viewpoint, Andrew R. Morral, Daniel F. McCaffrey, and Susan M. Paddock consider whether the correlation between marijuana use and hard drug use could be explained in a manner other than the gateway effect. While not disproving the gateway effect, the authors suggest an alternative explanation— the common-factor model—that could account for the phenomena often cited in support of the gateway effect. They claim the evidence for a marijuana gateway effect is currently inconclusive. Andrew R. Morral is director of the Safety and Justice Program at the RAND Institute, a nonprofit institution that is committed to improving public policy through research and analysis. Daniel F. McCaffrey and Susan M. Paddock are statisticians at RAND.

Andrew R. Morral, Daniel F. McCaffrey, and Susan M. Paddock, "Reassessing the Marijuana Gateway Effect," *Addiction*, vol. 97, December 2002, pp. 1493–1504. Copyright © 2002 Society for the Study of Addiction to Alcohol and other Drugs. Reproduced by permission of Blackwell Publishers.

As you read, consider the following questions:

1. What three phenomena does Morral claim are often cited in support of a gateway effect of marijuana?

2. Why does Morral argue that the three phenomena are not sufficient to prove a gateway effect?

3. According to Morral, how does the common-factor model account for each of the phenomena usually cited in support of the gateway effect?

Alcohol, tobacco and marijuana are widely regarded as "gateway" drugs. Although the gateway concept admits a number of definitions, one in particular predominates in drug policy discussions: use of gateway drugs causes youths to have an increased risk of progressing to other, more serious drugs. For instance, in debates on marijuana decriminalization or the medicinal use of marijuana, policy makers frequently suggest that use of marijuana increases youths' risk of initiating more dangerous drugs such as cocaine and heroin. Although marijuana is the least prevalent of the three principal gateway drugs, it is currently the focus of extensive policy reassessment in the United States, Canada, Western Europe and Australia. [We] demonstrate that the primary evidence supporting the marijuana gateway effect can be explained completely by the order in which youths first have the opportunity to use marijuana and other drugs, and by assuming a non-specific liability to use drugs, without any assumption that use of marijuana contributes to the risk of initiating use of hard drugs. We argue that although marijuana gateway effects may truly exist, available evidence does not favor the marijuana gateway effect over the alternative hypothesis that marijuana and hard drug initiation are correlated because both are influenced by individuals' heterogeneous liabilities to try drugs.

Three Phenomena Cited in Support of a Gateway Effect

The popular concern that marijuana use increases the risk of progressing to other, more serious drugs is a long-standing one, and has influenced US drug policy since at least the 1950s. Some social scientists have also suggested that marijuana gateway effects probably account for several phenomena observed in adolescent drug use initiation patterns Three such phenomena represent the primary evidence for a marijuana gateway effect. The first concerns the *relative risk* of hard drug initiation for adolescent marijuana users vs. non-users. In general, marijuana users in many countries appear to have a significantly elevated risk for drug use progression. Indeed, one US study found their risk to be 85 times those of non-users of marijuana. Another form of relative risk that is occasionally cited in support of the gateway effect is that younger marijuana initiates have a higher risk of initiating hard drug use than older marijuana initiates. This relative risk differs from the first only insofar as it finds that risk of hard drug initiation is conditioned on a characteristics of the user (age), rather than on marijuana use alone. Therefore, it does not provide strong evidence supporting a gateway effect.

The second observation routinely cited in support of the marijuana gateway effect concerns the remarkably invariant *ordering* in adolescents' initiation of different drug classes. Adolescents rarely initiate hard drug use before marijuana. For instance, in a longitudinal sample of 1265 New Zealand youths between the ages of 15 and 21, [D.M.] Fergusson & [L.J.] Horwood (2000) found only three cases reporting use of hard drugs before marijuana. This figure is dramatically lower than the roughly 124 such cases that would be expected from annual incidence rates if use of marijuana and hard drugs were independent.

The third phenomenon used to support claims of a marijuana gateway effect concerns the strong relationship between the frequency of marijuana consumption and the risk of hard drug initiation: as the frequency of marijuana use increases, so too does the risk of initiating hard drug use. Fergusson & Horwood (2000) for instance, developed a proportional haz-

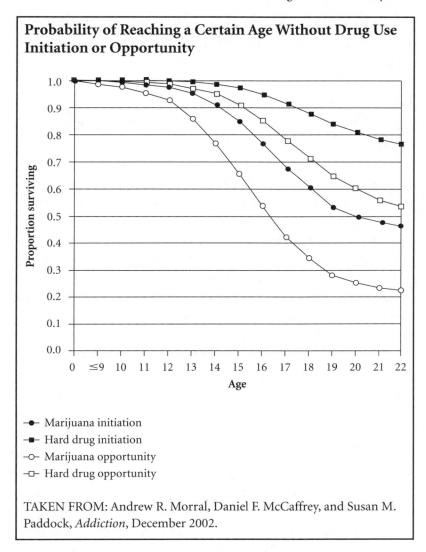

Probability of Reaching a Certain Age Without Drug Use Initiation or Opportunity

—●— Marijuana initiation
—■— Hard drug initiation
—○— Marijuana opportunity
—□— Hard drug opportunity

TAKEN FROM: Andrew R. Morral, Daniel F. McCaffrey, and Susan M. Paddock, *Addiction*, December 2002.

ards model suggested that youths reporting 50 or more uses of cannabis in the past year had hazards of progression to hard drugs that were more than 140 times greater than those for youths reporting no use of cannabis. Findings like this suggest an even stronger form of the marijuana gateway effect defined earlier: not only does marijuana use increase youths' risk of hard drug initiation, but every instance of marijuana use adds to that risk. For convenience, we refer to this phenomenon as marijuana's apparent *dose-response effect* on hard drug initiation.

The Common-Factor Model

The three phenomena of relative risk, ordering in drug use initiation and dose-response are not sufficient to prove that use of marijuana, rather than some associated factor, increases the risk of hard drug initiation. Indeed, a frequently cited alternative explanation is that a common factor, which we might refer to generically as a propensity for drug use, could influence use of both marijuana and hard drugs, thereby causing initiation of these drugs to be correlated. For instance, if high drug use propensities elevate individuals' risk for use of both marijuana and hard drugs, this could explain why marijuana users have a higher relative risk of hard drug initiation in comparison with non-users.

This 'common-factor' model does not immediately account for the ordering and dose-response phenomena. To make sense of these observations, proponents of the common-factor approach suggest that ordering in drug use initiation results from the order in which opportunities to use marijuana and hard drugs are presented to young people. Those with the highest propensities to use drugs are likely to use the first one offered to them, and that happens to be marijuana in most cases. Moreover, if a high drug use propensity is associated with greater frequencies of drug use, the common-factor theory can also account for the dose-response phenomenon: marijuana use frequency is associated with risk of hard drug initiation because both are controlled by drug use propensity.

The common-factor model is appealing in part because it takes account of what is a substantial scientific literature demonstrating the existence of genetic, familial and environmental characteristics associated with a generalized risk of using both marijuana and hard drugs. For instance, several studies examining drug use among monozygotic and dizygotic twins in the USA demonstrate genetic and family environment contributions to the likelihood of any drug use and any drug use initiation. Similarly, community drug use or drug availability may contribute to individuals' risk of using drugs.

Although the common-factor model is plausible, previous research has not demonstrated that propensities to use drugs and environmental factors such as drug use opportunities could, in fact, account for the strong relative risk, ordering and dose-response phenomena observed among adolescents. Indeed, [some] lines of model cannot account for drug use initiation without assuming a marijuana gateway effect. . . .

Gateway Effect Inconclusive

A simple common-factor model with population-based parameters can reproduce each of the phenomena previously used to support claims of a marijuana gateway effect. Thus, the strong relative risk, ordering and dose—response relationships observed between marijuana use and hard drug initiation do not require an assumption that marijuana initiation, or even the first opportunity to use it, increases the risk of either hard drug initiation or the opportunity to use hard drugs. While not disproving the existence of a marijuana gateway effect, our findings demonstrate that the primary evidence supporting gateway effects is equally consistent with an alternative model of adolescent drug use initiation in which use, *per se*, of marijuana has no effect on the later use of hard drugs.

Once a general propensity to use drugs is posited, the relative risk of hard drug use among marijuana users vs. non-users can be completely accounted for as a simple consequence of the fact that users of any drug are likely to have higher drug use propensities than non-users. Indeed, our model produced hard drug initiation risk ratios greater than those observed in the NHSDA [National Household Survey of

Drug Abuse] both for users vs. non-users of marijuana and for younger vs. older initiates of marijuana.

With the assumption that use of any drug is conditioned only on an individual's age, drug use propensity and opportunity to use drugs, the observed ordering in drug initiation can be attributed to the fact that opportunities to use marijuana routinely precede opportunities to use hard drugs—often by many years. Using just these assumptions, our model produced rates of hard drug use preceding marijuana use of just 11 per 1000 individuals, reflecting an even more invariant ordering than that found in our NHSDA sample, in which 16 of every 1000 individuals try hard drugs before marijuana.

Finally, even without the reasonable assumption of a correlation between marijuana use intensity and the more general propensity to use drugs, the assumptions of the model suffice to produce a strong dose-response relationship between marijuana use frequency and the risk of hard drug initiation. However, introducing such a correlation strengthens the dose-response relationship considerably. Indeed, as demonstrated by our sensitivity analysis, adjustments to the correlation between marijuana use intensity and drug use propensity suffice to account for the magnitude of the dose—response relationship observed for populations of youths. Again, the observed dose-response relationship between marijuana use frequency and the risk of hard drug initiation requires no marijuana gateway effect for its explanation.

> "It's rarely clear what people mean when
> they say that pot smoking leads to the
> use of 'harder' drugs."

The Meaning of the Gateway Drug Theory Is Ambiguous

Jacob Sullum

In the following viewpoint, Jacob Sullum argues that the main reason the gateway theory continues to be seen as a tenable theory is not due to overwhelming support by research, but due to the ambiguity of what the theory actually entails. Sullum argues that it is unclear whether the information used to justify the claim that marijuana has a gateway effect supports an effect that comes from marijuana itself, from its legal status, or from something about the user. Jacob Sullum is a senior editor of Reason, the libertarian monthly magazine.

As you read, consider the following questions:

1. What survey data does Sullum identify as having multiple interpretations?

2. What alternate explanation does Sullum offer for why one twin used marijuana and other illegal drugs, while the other did not?

3. In what three ways does Sullum suggest marijuana's status as an illegal drug may contribute to the gateway effect?

By the 1950s, Federal Bureau of Narcotics Commissioner Harry Anslinger had backed away from his claim that marijuana turns people into murderers. Instead he began arguing that it turns them into heroin addicts. "Over 50 percent of those young addicts started on marijuana smoking," Anslinger told a congressional committee in 1951. "They started there and graduated to heroin; they took the needle when the thrill of marijuana was gone."

Half a century later, this idea, known as the "gateway" or "stepping stone" theory, remains a bulwark of marijuana prohibition. Its durability is largely due to its ambiguity: Because it's rarely clear what people mean when they say that pot smoking leads to the use of "harder" drugs, the claim is difficult to disprove.

Interpreting the Data

Survey data indicate that heroin and cocaine users generally use marijuana first, and that people who try pot are much more likely than people who don't to try other drugs. But there are several ways of interpreting these facts. A recent study by the RAND Corporation's Drug Policy Research Center, for example, found that a general predisposition to use drugs, combined with a four-year lag between access to marijuana and access to other illegal intoxicants, was enough to account for the patterns observed in the government's surveys.

"The people who are predisposed to use drugs and have the opportunity to use drugs are more likely than others to use both marijuana and other drugs," said Andrew Morral, the lead author of the study, which appeared in the December issue of the journal *Addiction*. "Marijuana typically comes first because it is more available. Once we incorporated these facts into our mathematical model of adolescent drug use, we could explain all of the drug use associations that have been cited as evidence of marijuana's gateway effect."

Case closed? Not quite, A study reported in this week's *Journal of the American Medical Association* surveyed 311 pairs of Australian twins in which one used marijuana by age 17 and one did not. The researchers found that the early cannabis users were more likely than their twins to use other drugs. They were four times as likely to use psychedelics, three times as likely to use cocaine or other stimulants, and more than twice as likely to use opioids.

An Alternate Explanation

These relative probabilities may sound impressive, but they're quite modest compared to the numbers usually cited by defenders of the war on drugs. The prohibitionist propaganda mill known as the Center on Addiction and Substance Abuse, for example, trumpets the fact that "12-to-17-year-olds who smoke marijuana are 85 times more likely to use cocaine than those who do not." The results of the twin study suggest that almost all of this difference is due to environmental and personality factors, as indicated by RAND's analysis.

Even with twins, of course, there are differences in environment and personality. The study's results were similar for monozygotic ("identical") and dizygotic ("fraternal") twins, which suggests that genetic differences of the magnitude seen in siblings are not important in determining who uses the "harder" drugs. But both kinds of twins clearly differed in significant respects; otherwise, it would not have been the case that one from each pair used marijuana early while the other did not. If one twin happens to be less risk-averse or more rebellious, or if he happens to have friends who know where to get pot, that factor could explain both his early marijuana use and his subsequent use of other drugs.

Alternate Explanations for the Gateway Effect

Other mechanisms that might mediate a causal association between early cannabis use and subsequent drug use and drug abuse/dependence include the following.

Initial experiences with cannabis, which are frequently rated as pleasurable, may encourage continued use of cannabis and also broader experimentation.

Seemingly safe early experiences with cannabis may reduce the perceived risk of, and therefore barriers to, the use of other drugs. . . .

Alternatively, experience with and subsequent access to cannabis use may provide individuals with access to other drugs as they come into contact with drug dealers. . . .

While the findings of this study indicate that early cannabis use is associated with increased risks of progression to other illicit drug use and drug abuse/dependence, it is not possible to draw strong causal conclusions solely on the basis of the associations shown in this study. Further research in other cultures and using a range of innovative research designs (including evaluation of prevention efforts aimed at delaying the onset of cannabis use) is needed to explore whether there is a causal link between early cannabis use and progression to other drug use and, if so, to elucidate the mechanisms that may underlie any such causal association.

Source: Michael T. Lynskey, et al,
"Escalation of Drug Use in
Early-Onset Cannabis Users vs. Co-twin Controls,"
The Journal of the American Medical Association *(JAMA),*
January 22/29, 2003.

The researchers, for their part, speculated that the link between early pot smoking and later drug use "may arise from the effects of the peer and social context within which cannabis is used and obtained. In particular, early access to and use of cannabis may reduce perceived barriers against the use of other illegal drugs and provide access to these drugs."

What Causes the Gateway Effect?

To expand on that point a bit, the government's decision to put marijuana in the same category as cocaine and heroin may contribute to a gateway effect in three ways:

1. Once teenagers break the law to try pot, they are less reluctant to break the law to try other drugs.

2. Once they discover that the government has been lying about marijuana, they are less inclined to believe official warnings about other drugs.

3. Once they buy marijuana on the black market, they are more likely to have the opportunity to buy other drugs.

A more obvious explanation for the connection between pot smoking and other drug use is that people who discover that they like marijuana may be more inclined to try other psychoactive substances, in the same way that people who discover that they like bungee jumping may be more inclined to try sky diving. You could say that bungee jumping is a gateway to sky diving.

Notice that none of these interpretations involves a specific pharmacological effect of the sort drug warriors seem to have in mind when they suggest that pot smoking primes the brain for cocaine or heroin. As a National Academy of Sciences panel observed in a 1999 report, "There is no evidence that marijuana serves as a stepping stone on the basis of its particular drug effect." Last year the Canadian Senate's Special Committee on Illegal Drugs likewise concluded that "cannabis itself is not a cause of other drug use. In this scene, we reject the gateway theory."

Of course, it all depends on which "sense" you have in mind. A few year ago in the *Drug Policy Analysis Bulletin*, the social psychologist Robert MacCoun laid out seven—count 'em, seven—different versions of the gateway theory. "Given our current state of knowledge," he concluded, "one can coherently argue that (a) the gateway is a myth—it doesn't exist; (b) the gateway is very real and it shows why we must sustain or strengthen our ban on marijuana, or (c) the gateway is very real and it shows why we should depenalize or even legalize marijuana."

A theory that versatile will never die.

Periodical Bibliography

The following articles have been selected to supplement the diverse views presented in this chapter.

Brian C. Bennett   "Assessing the Marijuana 'Gateway' Theory," *BBS News*, January 15, 2003.

Scott Burns   "An Open Letter to America's Prosecutors," *Office of National Drug Control Policy*, 2002.

Kelly N. Graves et al.   "Risk and Protective Factors Associated with Alcohol, Cigarette, and Marijuana Use During Adolescence," *Journal of Youth and Adolescence*, August 2005.

Denise B. Kandel   "Alcohol and Cannabis May Be Gateway Drugs
and Kevin Chen   for Teens," *The Brown University Digest of Addiction Theory and Application*, April 2004.

Deborah Orr   "Are We Tolerating the Wrong Drugs?" *The Independent*, March 13, 2002.

George Sanju and   "'Gateway Hypothesis'—A Preliminary Evalua-
Moselhy Hamdy   tion of Variables Predicting Non-conformity," *Addictive Disorders and Their Treatment*, March 2005.

*Sarasota   "Beyond the Gateway: White House Should
Herald Tribune*   Reconcile Meth Policy with Congress' Concerns," August 29, 2005.

Fernando A. Wagner   "From First Drug Use to Drug Dependence:
and James C. Anthony   Developmental Periods of Risk for Dependence upon Marijuana, Cocaine, and Alcohol," *Neuropsychopharmacology*, 2002.

Fernando A. Wagner   "Male-Female Differences in the Risk of Pro-
and James C. Anthony   gression from First Use to Dependence upon Cannabis, Cocaine, and Alcohol," *Drug & Alcohol Dependence*, 2007.

OPPOSING
VIEWPOINTS®
SERIES

CHAPTER 2

Are Gateway Drugs Harmful?

Chapter Preface

When individuals make claims about certain drugs having a gateway effect, it is usually as part of a bigger argument in favor of restrictions on access to those drugs. The Drug Abuse Resistance Education program, commonly known as D.A.R.E., cites support for the theory "that the use of tobacco and alcohol is an indicator of subsequent illicit drug use among youth" as part of the justification for the importance of preventing young people from using tobacco and alcohol. Concern about a drug's status as a gateway drug aside, many argue that tobacco, alcohol, and marijuana are harmful in their own right, whether or not they lead to the use of other drugs.

People often distinguish between *soft* and *hard* drugs, though there are no definitive criteria for distinguishing a drug as hard or soft. The so-called gateway drugs of tobacco, alcohol, and marijuana are often referred to as soft drugs, with the concern that they provide a gateway to hard drugs, such as cocaine and heroin. The Narcotics Act of the Netherlands distinguishes between drugs that pose an unacceptable risk to public health—hard drugs—and those where the risk is acceptable enough to allow regulated use—soft drugs. Under the Act, Netherlands classifies heroin, cocaine, ecstasy, and methamphetamine as hard drugs while classifying marijuana, alcohol, and tobacco as soft drugs. Consequently, unlike the United States the Netherlands allows regulated use of marijuana. Like the United States, the Netherlands allows the regulated use of alcohol and tobacco, while prohibiting the use of heroin, cocaine, ecstasy, and methamphetamine.

Since alcohol and tobacco are legal in the United States, one may expect that these drugs are not as harmful as illegal drugs. As the debate among the authors in this chapter shows, this is far from settled. Additionally, while many refer to marijuana as a soft drug and call for its legalization, there is no consensus on the harmfulness of marijuana. Authors examine this issue of the harmfulness of tobacco, alcohol, and marijuana further in the following chapter. Determining whether certain drugs pose dangers in themselves—determining whether they are hard or soft—is relevant to considering drug policy, as is assessing whether the drugs have a gateway effect, leading to the use of other drugs.

| "*Marijuana available today is more potent than ever.*"

Marijuana Use Has Many Harmful Effects

Office of National Drug Control Policy

In the following viewpoint, the Office of National Drug Control Policy identifies several myths about marijuana safety. The Office of National Drug Control Policy argues that marijuana is not harmless; it is addictive; it is harmful like tobacco; it makes people violent; and it does not show medical benefits that outweigh harms. The White House Office of National Drug Control Policy was established by the Anti-Drug Abuse Act of 1988 with the purpose of establishing policies, priorities, and objectives for the nation's drug control program.

As you read, consider the following questions:

1. According to the Office of National Drug Policy, what are four short-term effects of marijuana use?
2. What percentage of Americans was classified with dependence on or abuse of marijuana, according to a 2002 survey?

Office of National Drug Control Policy, *Marijuana Myths & Facts: The Truth Behind Ten Popular Misperceptions*, 2004.

3. What evidence does the Office of National Drug Policy point to in order to argue that marijuana makes people violent or aggressive?

Marijuana harms in many ways, and kids are the most vulnerable to its damaging effects. Use of the drug can lead to significant health, safety, social, and learning or behavioral problems, especially for young users. Making matters worse is the fact that the marijuana available today is more potent than ever.

Myth: Marijuana Is Harmless

Short-term effects of marijuana use include memory loss, distorted perception, trouble with thinking and problem-solving, and anxiety. Students who use marijuana may find it hard to learn, thus jeopardizing their ability to achieve their full potential.

Cognitive impairment: That marijuana can cause problems with concentration and thinking has been shown in research funded by the National Institute on Drug Abuse (NIDA), the federal agency that brings the power of science to bear on drug abuse and addiction. A NIDA-funded study at McLean Hospital in Belmont, Massachusetts, is part of the growing body of research documenting cognitive impairment among heavy marijuana users. The study found that college students who used marijuana regularly had impaired skills related to attention, memory, and learning 24 hours after they last used the drug.

Another study, conducted at the University of Iowa College of Medicine, found that people who used marijuana frequently (7 or more times weekly for an extended period) showed deficits in mathematical skills and verbal expression, as well as selective impairments in memory-retrieval processes. These findings clearly have significant implications for young people, since reductions in cognitive function can lead to poor performance in school.

Other impairments observed in frequent marijuana users involve sensory and time perception and coordinated movement, suggesting use of the drug can adversely affect driving and sports performance. Effects such as these may be especially problematic during teens' peak learning years, when their brains are still developing.

Mental health problems: Smoking marijuana leads to changes in the brain similar to those caused by cocaine, heroin, and alcohol. All of these drugs disrupt the flow of chemical neurotransmitters, and all have specific receptor sites in the brain that have been linked to feelings of pleasure and, over time, addiction. Cannabinoid receptors are affected by THC, the active ingredient in marijuana, and many of these sites are found in the parts of the brain that influence pleasure, memory, thought, concentration, sensory and time perception, and coordinated movement.

Particularly for young people, marijuana use can lead to increased anxiety, panic attacks, depression, and other mental health problems. One study linked social withdrawal, anxiety, depression, attention problems, and thoughts of suicide in adolescents with past-year marijuana use. Other research shows that kids age 12 to 17 who smoke marijuana weekly are three times more likely than non-users to have thoughts about committing suicide. A recently published longitudinal study showed that use of cannabis increased the risk of major depression fourfold, and researchers in Sweden found a link between marijuana use and an increased risk of developing schizophrenia.

According to the American Society of Addiction Medicine, addiction and psychiatric disorders often occur together. The latest National Survey on Drug Use and Health reported that adults who use illicit drugs were more than twice as likely to have serious mental illness as adults who did not use an illicit drug.

Researchers conducting a longitudinal study of psychiatric disorders and substance use (including alcohol, marijuana, and other illicit drugs) have suggested several possible links between the two: 1) people may use drugs to feel better and alleviate symptoms of a mental disorder; 2) the use of the drug and the disorder share certain biological, social, or other risk factors; or 3) use of the drug can lead to anxiety, depression, or other disorders.

Traffic safety: Marijuana also harms when it contributes to auto crashes or other incidents that injure or kill, a problem that is especially prevalent among young people. In a study reported by the National Highway Traffic Safety Administration, even a moderate dose of marijuana was shown to impair driving performance. The study measured reaction time and how often drivers checked the rear-view mirror, side streets, and the relative speed of other vehicles.

Another study looked at data concerning shock-trauma patients who had been involved in traffic crashes. The researchers found that 15 percent of the trauma patients who were injured while driving a car or motorcycle had been smoking marijuana, and another 17 percent had both THC and alcohol in their blood. Statistics such as these are particularly troubling in light of recent survey results indicating that almost 36 million people age 12 or older drove under the influence of alcohol, marijuana, or another illicit drug in the past year.

Long-term consequences: The consequences of marijuana use can last long after the drug's effects have worn off. Studies show that early use of marijuana is strongly associated with later use of other illicit drugs and with a greater risk of illicit drug dependence or abuse. In fact, an analysis of data from the National Household Survey on Drug Abuse showed that the age of initiation for marijuana use was the most important predictor of later need for drug treatment.

"Wish I Could!" cartoon by Ray Jelliffe, CartoonStock.com.

Regular marijuana use has been shown to be associated with other long-term problems, including poor academic performance, poor job performance and increased absences from work, cognitive deficits, and lung damage. Marijuana use is also associated with a number of risky sexual behaviors, including having multiple sex partners, initiating sex at an early age, and failing to use condoms consistently.

Myth: Marijuana Is Not Addictive

It was once believed that marijuana was not addictive; many people still believe this to be the case. But recent research shows that use of the drug can indeed lead to dependence. Some heavy users of marijuana develop withdrawal symptoms when they have not used the drug for a period of time.

Marijuana use, in fact, is often associated with behavior that meets the criteria for substance dependence established by the American Psychiatric Association in the *Diagnostic and Statistical Manual of Mental Disorders* (DSM-IV). Considered the standard reference for health professionals who make psychiatric diagnoses, the DSM contains information about all mental disorders for children and adults. As described in the DSM, the criteria for substance dependence include tolerance (needing more of the substance to achieve the same effects, or diminished effect with the same amount of the substance); withdrawal symptoms; using a drug even in the presence of adverse effects; and giving up social, occupational, or recreational activities because of substance use. According to the 2002 National Survey on Drug Use and Health, 4.3 million Americans were classified with dependence on or abuse of marijuana. That figure represents 1.8 percent of the total U.S. population and 60.3 percent of those classified as individuals who abuse or are dependent on illicit drugs.

The desire for marijuana exerts a powerful pull on those who use it, and this desire, coupled with withdrawal symptoms, can make it hard for long-term smokers to stop using the drug. Users trying to quit often report irritability, anxiety, and difficulty sleeping. On psychological tests they also display increased aggression, which peaks approximately one week after they last used the drug.

Many people use marijuana compulsively even though it interferes with family, school, work, and recreational activities. What makes this all the more disturbing is that marijuana use has been shown to be three times more likely to lead to dependence among adolescents than among adults. Research indicates that the earlier kids start using marijuana, the more likely they are to become dependent on this or other illicit drugs later in life.

Treatment admissions: More teens enter treatment each year with a primary diagnosis of marijuana dependence than for all other illicit drugs combined. Currently, 62 percent of teens in drug treatment are dependent on marijuana.

The proportion of admissions for primary marijuana abuse increased from 6 percent in 1992 to 15 percent of admissions to treatment in 2000. Almost half (47 percent) of the people admitted for marijuana were under 20 years old, and many of them started smoking pot at a very early age. Of those admitted for treatment for primary marijuana dependence, 56 percent had first used the drug by age 14, and 26 percent had begun by age 12.

Myth: Marijuana Is Not as Harmful as Tobacco

Although some people think of marijuana as a benign natural herb, the drug actually contains many of the same cancer-causing chemicals found in tobacco. Puff for puff, the amount of tar inhaled and the level of carbon monoxide absorbed by those who smoke marijuana, regardless of THC content, are three to five times greater than among tobacco smokers.

Consequently, people who use marijuana on a regular basis often have the same breathing problems as tobacco users, such as chronic coughing and wheezing, more frequent acute chest illnesses, and a tendency toward obstructed airways. And because respiratory problems can affect athletic performance, smoking marijuana may be particularly harmful to kids involved in sports.

Researchers at the University of California, Los Angeles, have determined that marijuana smoking can cause potentially serious damage to the respiratory system at a relatively early age. Moreover, in a review of research on the health effects of marijuana use, the researchers cited findings that show "the daily smoking of relatively small amounts of marijuana (3 to 4 joints) has at least a comparable, if not greater effect" on the respiratory system than the smoking of more than 20 tobacco cigarettes.

Recently, scientists in England produced further evidence linking marijuana use to respiratory problems in young people. A research team at the University of Birmingham found that regular use of marijuana, even for less than six years, causes a marked deterioration in lung function. These findings, the study concludes, "may have serious long-term implications for what is currently regarded as a relatively 'harmless' recreational habit."

Myth: Marijuana Makes You Mellow

Not always. Research shows that kids who use marijuana weekly are nearly four times more likely than non-users to report they engage in violent behavior. One study found that young people who had used marijuana in the past year were more likely than non-users to report aggressive behavior. According to that study, incidences of physically attacking people, stealing, and destroying property increased in proportion to the number of days marijuana was smoked in the past year. Users were also twice as likely as non-users to report they disobey at school and destroy their own things.

In another study, researchers looking into the relationship between ten illicit drugs and eight criminal offenses found that a greater frequency of marijuana use was associated with a greater likelihood to commit weapons offenses; except for alcohol, none of the other drugs showed such a connection. That study, published in the *Journal of Addictive Diseases* in 2001, also found a link between marijuana use and the commission of attempted homicide and reckless endangerment offenses.

Marijuana Is Used to Treat Cancer and Other Diseases

Under the Comprehensive Drug Abuse Prevention and Control Act of 1970, marijuana was established as a Schedule I controlled substance. In other words, it is a dangerous drug that has no recognized medical value.

Whether marijuana can provide relief for people with certain medical conditions, including cancer, is a subject of intense national debate. It is true that THC, the primary active chemical in marijuana, can be useful for treating some medical problems. Synthetic THC is the main ingredient in Marinol®, an FDA-approved medication used to control nausea in cancer chemotherapy patients and to stimulate appetite in people with AIDS. Marinol, a legal and safe version of medical marijuana, has been available by prescription since 1985.

However, marijuana as a smoked product has never proven to be medically beneficial and, in fact, is much more likely to harm one's health; marijuana smoke is a crude THC delivery system that also sends many harmful substances into the body. In 1999, the Institute of Medicine (IOM) published a review of the available scientific evidence in an effort to assess the potential health benefits of marijuana and its constituent cannabinoids. The review concluded that smoking marijuana is not recommended for any long-term medical use, and a subsequent IOM report declared, "marijuana is not a modern medicine."

Clinical trials of smoked marijuana for therapy are underway through the National Institutes of Health, a major provider of funding for research on the potential medical uses of marijuana. Meanwhile, the best available evidence points to the conclusion that the adverse effects of marijuana smoke on the respiratory system would almost certainly offset any possible benefit.

Some states have removed criminal penalties for possessing marijuana for "medical" use, adding fuel to the debate about using smoked marijuana to reduce suffering. Residents in those states have voted to change the marijuana policy in the mistaken belief that the benefits of smoked marijuana exceed those provided by THC alone. A number of organizations are pushing to make marijuana available for medicinal purposes, but this campaign is regarded by many public-health experts as a veiled effort to legalize the drug.

Moreover, medicines are not approved in this country by popular vote. Before any drugs can be released for public use they must undergo rigorous clinical trials to demonstrate they are both safe and effective, and then be approved by the Food and Drug Administration. Our investment and confidence in medical science will be seriously undermined if we do not defend the proven process by which medicines are brought to market.

| "Marijuana's relative risk to the user
and society does not support criminal
prohibition."

The Harmful Effects of
Marijuana Are Minimal

Paul Armentano

*In the following viewpoint, Paul Armentano argues that there
have been numerous allegations made about the harms of marijuana that are not true. In this selection, Armentano presents his
refutation of seven different claims about the harmfulness of
marijuana, including worries about its effect on the brain, its
addictiveness, and its role in causing violence. Paul Armentano
has served for over ten years as a researcher and policy analyst
for the National Organization for the Reform of Marijuana
Laws (NORML) in Washington, D.C.*

As you read, consider the following questions:

1. Why is marijuana use not a significant factor in emergency room visits, according to the author?

Paul Armentano, *The 2005 NORML Truth Report: Your Government Is Lying To You
(Again) About Marijuana*, Washington, DC: The National Organization for the Reform
of Marijuana Laws (NORML), 2005. http://norml.org. Copyright © 2005 NORML. Reproduced by permission.

2. According to the Institute of Medicine report that Armentano cites, how does the percentage of dependent marijuana users compare with the percentages of dependent alcohol, cocaine, and tobacco users?

3. According to the author, which substance do scientific studies show contributes more to violent behavior, marijuana or alcohol?

A *llegation: "The truth is that marijuana is not harmless."*

This statement is correct; marijuana isn't harmless. In fact, no substance is, including those that are legal. However, any risk presented by marijuana smoking falls within the ambit of choice we permit the individual in a free society. According to federal statistics, approximately 80 million Americans self-identify as having used marijuana at some point in their lives, and relatively few acknowledge having suffered significant deleterious health effects due to their use. America's public policies should reflect this reality, not deny it.

Marijuana's relative risk to the user and society does not support criminal prohibition or the continued arrest of more than 750,000 Americans on marijuana charges every year. As concluded by the Canadian House of Commons in their December 2002 report recommending marijuana decriminalization, "The consequences of conviction for possession of a small amount of cannabis for personal use are disproportionate to the potential harm associated with the behavior."

Allegation: "As a factor in emergency room visits, marijuana has risen 176 percent since 1994, and now surpasses heroin."

This statement is intentionally misleading as it wrongly suggests that marijuana use is a significant causal factor in an alarming number of emergency room visits. It is not.

Federal statistics gathered by the Drug Abuse Warning Network (DAWN) do indicate an increase in the number of people "mentioning" marijuana during hospital emergency room visits. (This increase is hardly unique to marijuana however, as the overall number of drug mentions has risen dramatically since the late 1980s—likely due to improved federal reporting procedures.) However, a marijuana "mention" does not mean that marijuana caused the hospital visit or that it was a factor in leading to the ER episode, only that the patient said that he or she had used marijuana previously.

For every emergency room visit related to drug use (so-called "drug abuse episodes"), hospital staff list up to five drugs the patient reports having used recently, regardless of whether or not their use of the drug caused the visit. The frequency with which any drug is mentioned in such visits is generally proportional to its frequency of use, irrespective of its inherent dangers.

It is foolish for anyone—especially those in the administration's anti-drug office—to imply that marijuana is in any way potentially more dangerous to one's health than heroin. Marijuana is mentioned to hospital staff more frequently than heroin, not because it's more dangerous, but simply because a far greater percentage of the population uses marijuana than uses heroin. It is also worth noting that alcohol is by far the drug most frequently reported to DAWN, even though it is reported only when present in combination with another reportable drug. Moreover, marijuana is rarely mentioned independent of other drugs.

Allegation: "Smoked marijuana leads to changes in the brain similar to those caused by the use of cocaine and heroin."

Allegations that marijuana smoking alters brain function or has long-term effects on cognition are reckless and scientifically unfounded. Federally sponsored population studies conducted in Jamaica, Greece and Costa Rica found no significant differences in brain function between long-term smokers and non-users. Similarly, a 1999 study of 1,300 volunteers published in *The American Journal of Epidemiology* reported "no significant differences in cognitive decline between heavy users, light users, and nonusers of cannabis" over a 15-year period. More recently, a meta-analysis of neuropsychological studies of long-term marijuana smokers by the National Institute on Drug Abuse reaffirmed this conclusion. In addition, a study published in the *Canadian Medical Association Journal* in April 2002 reported that even former heavy marijuana smokers experience no negative measurable effects on intelligence quotient.

Most recently, researchers at Harvard Medical School performed magnetic resonance imaging on the brains of 22 long-term cannabis users (reporting a mean of 20,100 lifetime episodes of smoking) and 26 controls (subjects with no history of cannabis use). Imaging displayed "no significant differences" between heavy cannabis smokers compared to controls. "These findings are consistent with recent literature suggesting that cannabis use is not associated with structural changes within the brain as a whole or the hippocampus in particular," authors concluded.

Claims specifically charging that marijuana leads to brain changes similar to those induced by heroin and cocaine are based solely on the results of a handful of animal studies that demonstrated that THC (delta-9-tetrahydrocannabinol, the main psychoactive ingredient in marijuana) can stimulate dopamine production under certain extreme conditions, and that the immediate cessation of THC (via the administration of a chemical blocking agent) will initiate some mild symptoms of withdrawal. These findings have little bearing on the human population because, according to the US Institute of Medicine, "The long half-life and slow elimination from the body of THC . . . prevent[s] substantial abstinence symptoms" in humans. As a result, such symptoms have only been identified in rare, unique patient settings—limited to adolescents in treatment for substance abuse, or in clinical research trials where volunteers are administered marijuana or THC daily.

Scare Tactics and Misinformation About Marijuana

In my travels I have conducted many workshops where parents question claims they've heard about marijuana. The most common are:

- Is it true that today's marijuana is significantly more potent than thirty or forty years ago [when they were teenagers]?

- Is today's marijuana really more addictive than ever before?

- Does marijuana really cause users to seek out "harder" drugs?

- Is it true that smoking marijuana causes lung cancer?

To separate myth from fact, (the late) Professor Lynn Zimmer of Queens College of the City University of New York and Dr. John P. Morgan of the City University of New York Medical School carefully examined the published, peer-reviewed scientific evidence relevant to the most popular claims about marijuana in their book, *Marijuana Myths, Marijuana Facts: A Review of the Scientific Evidence*. Professor Mitch Earleywine of the State University of New York at Albany also took a critical look at the research in *Understanding Marijuana: a New Look at the Scientific Evidence*. Each found that claims of marijuana's risks had been exaggerated, even in some instances fabricated. Their findings are not uncommon, as these same conclusions have been reached by numerous official commissions, including . . . the federally chartered Institute of Medicine in 1999.

Marsha Rosenbaum, PhD,
Safety First: A Reality-based Approach, *2007.*

Allegation: "One recent study involving a roadside check of reckless drivers (not impaired by alcohol) showed that 45 percent tested positive for marijuana."

Though portrayed by politicians and police as a serious problem bordering on "epidemic," actual data is sparse concerning the prevalence of motorists driving under the influence of drugs, and more importantly, what role illicit drug use plays in traffic accidents.

While it is well established that alcohol increases accident risk, evidence of marijuana's culpability in on-road driving accidents is less understood. Although marijuana intoxication has been shown to mildly impair psychomotor skills, this impairment does not appear to be severe or long lasting. In driving simulator tests, this impairment is typically manifested by subjects decreasing their driving speed and requiring greater time to respond to emergency situations.

This impairment *does not* appear to play a significant role in on-road traffic accidents when THC levels in a driver's blood are low and/or THC is not consumed in combination with alcohol. For example, a 1992 US National Highway Traffic Safety Administration review of fatally injured drivers found, "THC-only drivers [those with detectable levels of THC in their blood] had a responsibility rate below that of drug-free drivers." A 1993 study conducted by the Institute of Human Psychopharmacology at the University of Maastrict (the Netherlands) evaluating cannabis' effects on actual driving performance found, "THC in single inhaled doses . . . has significant, yet not dramatic, dose-related impairing effects on driving performance. . . . THC's effects on road-tracking . . . never exceeded alcohol's at BACs [blood-alcohol contents] of .08% and were in no way unusual compared to many medicinal drugs."

A 2002 review of seven separate crash culpability studies involving 7,934 drivers reported that "crash culpability studies [which attempt to correlate the responsibility of a driver for an accident to his or her consumption of a drug and the level of drug compound in his or her system] have failed to demonstrate that drivers with cannabinoids in the blood are significantly more likely than drug-free drivers to be culpable in road crashes."

More recently, a 2004 scientific review of driver impairment and motor vehicle crashes suggested that "recent cannabis use may increase crash risk, whereas, past use of cannabis as determined by the presence of THC-COOH (marijuana's inactive metabolite) in drivers does not." An additional review by Drummer and colleagues further suggested that higher THC blood levels—particularly those above 5 ng/ml, indicating that the cannabis use had likely been within the past 1–3 hours—may be correlated with an elevated accident risk, noting, "The odds ratio for THC concentrations of 5 ng/ml or higher [are] similar to those drivers with a BAC of at least 0.15%." However, a meta-analysis by a German research team of 87 experimental studies on cannabis did not find such elevated impairment, suggesting "that a THC level in blood serum of 5ng/ml ... produces the same overall reduction in test performance as does a BAC of 0.05%."

But, unlike with alcohol, the accident risk caused by cannabis—particularly among those who are not acutely intoxicated—appears limited because subjects under its influence are generally aware of their impairment and compensate to some extent, such as by slowing down and by focusing their attention when they know a response will be required. This response is the opposite of that exhibited by drivers under the influence of alcohol, who tend to drive in a more risky manner proportional to their intoxication.

In short, the quantitative role of cannabis consumption in on-road traffic accidents is, at this point, not well understood. However, marijuana does not appear to play a significant role in vehicle crashes, particularly when compared to alcohol. As summarized by the Canadian Senate's exhaustive 2002 report:

"Cannabis: Our Position for a Canadian Public Policy," "Cannabis alone, particularly in low doses, has little effect on the skills involved in automobile driving."

Allegation: "The truth is that marijuana is addictive. . . . Marijuana users have an addiction rate of about 10%, and of the 5.6 million drug users who are suffering from illegal drug dependence or abuse, 62 percent are dependent on or abusing marijuana."

Marijuana use is not marijuana abuse. According to the US Institute of Medicine's 1999 Report: "Marijuana and Medicine: Assessing the Science Base," "Millions of Americans have tried marijuana, but most are not regular users, . . . [and] few marijuana users become dependent on it." In fact, less than 10 percent of marijuana users ever exhibit symptoms of dependence (as defined by the American Psychiatric Association's DSM-IV criteria.) By comparison 15 percent of alcohol users, 17 percent of cocaine users, and a whopping 32 percent of cigarette smokers statistically exhibit symptoms of drug dependence.

Marijuana is well recognized as lacking the so-called "dependence liability" of other substances. According to the IOM, "Experimental animals that are given the opportunity to self administer cannabinoids generally do not choose to do so, which has led to the conclusion that they are not reinforcing or rewarding." Among humans, most marijuana users voluntarily cease their marijuana smoking by their late 20s or early 30s—often citing health or professional concerns and/or the decision to start a family. Contrast this pattern with that of the typical tobacco smoker—many of whom begin as teens and continue smoking daily the rest of their lives.

That's not to say that some marijuana smokers do not become psychologically dependent on marijuana or find quitting difficult. But a comprehensive study released in 2002 by the Canadian Senate concluded that this dependence "is less severe and less frequent than dependence on other psychotropic substances, including alcohol and tobacco." Observable withdrawal symptoms attributable to marijuana are also exceedingly rare. According to the Institute of Medicine, these symptoms are "mild and short lived" compared to the profound physical withdrawal symptoms of other drugs, such as alcohol or heroin, and unlikely to persuade former smokers to reinitiate their marijuana use.

Allegation: "Average THC levels rose from less than 1% in the late 1970s to more than 7% in 2001, and sinsemilla potency increased from 6% to 13%, and now reach as high as 33%."

This statement is both inaccurate and misleading. No population en masse has ever smoked marijuana averaging less than one percent THC since such low potency marijuana would not induce euphoria. In many nations, including Canada and the European Union, marijuana of one percent THC or less is legally classified as an agricultural fiber crop, hemp.

Although annual marijuana potency data compiled by the University of Mississippi's Research Institute of Pharmaceutical Sciences does show a slight increase in marijuana's strength through the years, this increase is not nearly as dramatic as purported by the White House Office of National Drug Control Policy. *In addition, quantities of exceptionally strong strains of marijuana or sinsemilla (seedless marijuana) comprise only a small percentage of the overall marijuana market.* The NIDA-sponsored Marijuana Potency Monitoring Project reports that less than 10 percent of DEA seized marijuana samples are above 15 percent. Less than 2 percent of marijuana seized from the domestic market contains more than 20% THC. Data from Europe also refutes claims of increased cannabis potency, concluding "the potencies of resin and herbal cannabis . . . have shown little or no change, at least over the past ten years." The drug czar's upper-level THC figures are clearly a scare tactic.

Moreover, it's worth noting that more potent marijuana is not necessarily more dangerous. Marijuana poses no risk of fatal overdose, regardless of THC content, and since marijuana's greatest potential health hazard stems from the user's intake of carcinogenic smoke, it may be argued that higher potency marijuana may be slightly less harmful because it permits people to achieve desired psychoactive effects while inhaling less burning material. In addition, studies indicate that marijuana smokers distinguish between high and low potency marijuana and moderate their use accordingly, just as an alcohol consumer would drink fewer ounces of (high potency) bourbon than they would ounces of (low potency) beer.

Allegation: "The truth is that marijuana and violence are linked."

Absolutely not. No credible research has shown marijuana use to play a causal factor in violence, aggression or delinquent behavior, dating back to former President Richard Nixon's "First Report of the National Commission on Marihuana and Drug Abuse" in 1972, which concluded, "In short, marihuana is not generally viewed by participants in the criminal justice community as a major contributing influence in the commission of delinquent or criminal acts."

More recently, the Canadian Senate's 2002 "Discussion Paper on Cannabis" reaffirmed: "Cannabis use does not induce users to commit other forms of crime. Cannabis use does not increase aggressiveness or anti-social behavior." In contrast, research has demonstrated that certain legal drugs, such as alcohol, do induce aggressive behavior.

"Cannabis differs from alcohol . . . in one major respect. It does not seem to increase risk-taking behavior," the British Advisory Council on the Misuse of Drugs concluded in its 2002 report recommending the depenalization of marijuana. "This means that cannabis rarely contributes to violence either to others or to oneself, whereas alcohol use is a major factor in deliberate self-harm, domestic accidents and violence."

Most recently, a logistical retrogression analysis of approximately 900 trauma patients by SUNY-Buffalo's Department of Family Medicine found that use of cannabis is not independently associated with either violent or non-violent injuries requiring hospitalization. Alcohol and cocaine use were associated with violence-related injuries, the study found. Accordingly, fewer than five percent of state and local law enforcement agencies identify marijuana as a drug that significantly contributes to violent crime in their areas.

| "There is no possible benefit which can be derived from the use of alcohol internally."

Alcohol Use Is Harmful

Albert S. Whiting

In the following viewpoint, Albert S. Whiting argues that alcohol has only negative effects on the body, harming the liver, heart, brain, digestive system, and reproductive system. In light of these harmful effects, and because he believes that there are no positive effects of alcohol, he concludes that consumption of alcohol should be completely avoided. Albert S. Whiting worked within the world health and temperance department of the General Conference of the Seventh-day Adventist Church for over twenty years, serving as assistant director and director.

As you read, consider the following questions:

1. According to the author, is alcohol a stimulant or a depressant?

2. What is the first portion of the brain to be affected, according to Whiting, and what results does this have for the drinker?

3. What harm can result from drinking during pregnancy, according to the author?

Albert S. Whiting, "Alcohol and the Body," Women's Christian Temperance Union. www.wctu.org/alcohol_and_the_body.html. Reproduced by permission.

Alcohol is the oldest and most widely used drug in the world. Primitive cultures believed alcohol to be a magical, mysterious cure for nearly every ailment. Clinical research has removed the mystery of what happens when a person drinks alcohol. We have learned a great deal about what alcohol is, what it does in the body, and how it affects behavior.

What It Is and How It Is Absorbed

Alcohol belongs to a family of chemicals that contain carbon and hydrogen. The active ingredient in alcoholic beverages is ethyl alcohol, also known as ethanol. It is a colorless and nearly tasteless liquid that is easily and quickly absorbed by the body.

Many people think alcohol is a stimulant, but actually it is a depressant. It slows down the function of all living cells, especially those in the brain. Alcohol belongs to the same group of drugs as anesthetics and tranquilizers.

Alcohol does not need to be digested after having been consumed. It moves with tremendous speed through the body, affecting every single tissue and organ. It quickly appears in the bloodstream, and its intoxicating effects are felt within a few minutes.

The body begins immediately to *try* to get rid of the alcohol. It is absorbed through the stomach or small intestine directly into the bloodstream. It then proceeds to the liver, where it is broken down or metabolized. . . .

However, when it is consumed at a faster rate than the body's metabolism can handle (about one 12-ounce can of beer per hour), alcohol accumulates in the bloodstream and is distributed throughout the body. The higher the concentration of alcohol, the greater the disturbance it has on body cells. Severe disruption of function can occur and can cause death. The effects of alcohol on various organs will be discussed in more detail below.

Effects of Alcohol on Parts of the Body

On the liver: Because the liver must perform most of the work of metabolizing alcohol, it bears the brunt of its effects. Even in the moderate drinker, after some years of continuous low-grade dysfunction, the damaged liver cells are gradually replaced by scar tissue. Irreversible scarring and destruction of the liver is known as cirrhosis of the liver.

As the liver becomes damaged, its ability to metabolize alcohol is reduced. The liver begins to accumulate fats, and there is further malfunction. The risk of other diseases such as hepatitis is increased.

On the heart: There have been reports that one drink a day slightly decreases the risk of heart disease because alcohol affects the way cholesterol is carried in the blood. However, there is a great deal of evidence to show that even a small amount of alcohol can be quite harmful to the heart.

Alcohol has a direct effect on heart muscle cells. It can progressively destroy heart muscle so the heart cannot pump efficiently. Alcohol also starves the heart by decreasing blood flow in the coronary arteries.

Alcohol has an influence on the risk factors for coronary heart disease. Drinkers have an increased rate of hypertension. Fat levels in the blood can be elevated by alcohol. And alcohol contains a great many calories, which can cause obesity and increase chances of heart disease.

Because of its sedative effects, alcohol depresses angina heart pains. If a person exercises after drinking and does not feel this pain, a heart attack may result.

On the brain: The organ most sensitive to alcohol is the brain. Alcohol affects the entire body, but its effects on the functions of the brain are the most noticeable—and to the person who is drinking, the most important. People drink alcohol because of the way it makes them feel, ignoring the damaging effects on the brain itself.

The Harms of Alcohol Use for Young People

Many people don't know that underage alcohol use—

- *Is a major cause of death from injuries among young people.* Each year, approximately 5,000 people under the age of 21 die as a result of underage drinking; this includes about 1,900 deaths from motor vehicle crashes, 1,600 as a result of homicides, 300 from suicide, as well as hundreds from other injuries such as falls, burns, and drownings.

- *Increases the risk of carrying out, or being a victim of, a physical or sexual assault.*

- *Can affect the body in many ways.* The effects of alcohol range from hangovers to death from alcohol poisoning.

- *Can lead to other problems.* These may include bad grades in school, run-ins with the law, and drug use.

- *Affects how well a young person judges risk and makes sound decisions.* For example, after drinking, a teen may see nothing wrong with driving a car or riding with a driver who has been drinking.

- *Plays a role in risky sexual activity.* This can increase the chance of teen pregnancy and sexually transmitted diseases (STDs), including HIV, the virus that causes AIDS.

- *Can harm the growing brain, especially when teens drink a lot.* Today we know that the brain continues to develop from birth through the teen years into the mid-20s.

U.S. Dept. of Health and Human Services,
The Surgeon General's Call to Action To Prevent and Reduce
Underage Drinking. A Guide for Communities, *2007.*

The brain reacts to alcohol in stages. The first portion of the brain to be affected is the cerebrum—the outermost layer, which is responsible for controlling the senses, speech, understanding, and judgement.

Alcohol depresses first the parts of the brain that normally inhibit or control actions and emotions. It appears as if alcohol—although it is a depressant—is acting as a stimulant because, as these higher centers of the brain are knocked out the drinker feels liberated from moral and legal restrictions. The loss of these restraints can cause exhilaration and loss of inhibitions.

The alcohol continues to depress brain functions, resulting in slurred speech, unsteady walk, blurry vision, and loss of coordination. Drinkers often feel that their manual skills have been improved because their judgment has been impaired, while in reality their reaction times are slowed and their muscle coordination is less efficient.

Next, the drinker experiences various exaggerations of the emotions that can range from violence and aggressiveness to tearfulness and withdrawal. If a person continues to drink, the body protects itself from further damage by falling asleep or "passing out".

Alcohol destroys brain cells which, unlike the blood cells it also destroys, are irreplaceable. Alcohol impairs the memory as well as the ability to learn new things.

On the digestive system: Alcohol has absolutely no nutritive value other than calories, called "empty calories" because of the body's inability to store them. In fact, alcohol could be called an anti-nutrient because it actually increases the need for other nutrients.

Because alcohol supplies calories, alcoholic drinks can be very fattening. Alcohol is absorbed so quickly that its energy is available almost immediately. This energy is burned first, so the body fuel that would normally be used for energy is instead stored as fat.

The gastrointestinal system is irritated and damaged by alcohol. Thus, it is less able to absorb nutrients, which can lead to malnutrition.

On the reproductive system: When a pregnant woman drinks alcohol, it is distributed throughout both her body and the body of her unborn child. The developing baby is very sensitive to toxic substances, and alcohol can cause irreparable damage.

Alcohol interferes with the flow of oxygen to the fetus. This can result in smaller babies, birth defects, and even miscarriage.

The set of defects caused by drinking alcohol while pregnant is called fetal alcohol syndrome (FAS). This includes a range of disabilities involving facial deformities, limb and cardiovascular defects and impaired intellectual and motor development.

FAS, retarded growth, and behavioral difficulties are seen in the children of women who have consumed as little as a drink or two per day. Women who go on binges and drink excessively on occasion run the greatest risk of having brain-impaired babies.

The evidence is overwhelmingly conclusive that the only safe policy is complete abstention from alcohol during pregnancy. It has been shown that alcohol is harmful to the human system. The only wise response is to avoid its use as a beverage.

Alcohol Tolerance

Regular drinking increases a person's tolerance for alcohol. More is needed to feel the same effects—the single drink which once produced a feeling of relaxation is soon increased to two, and so on. The slide from drinking for pleasure to dependence is gradual.

The body tries to adapt to chronic alcohol use—the liver attempts to metabolize the alcohol more quickly, the cells work harder to get rid of it, and the drinker's behavior adapts to disguise impaired abilities. But after a while the body can no longer maintain equilibrium, and many organs become dysfunctional and permanently damaged.

Alcohol is not an antidote for snake bite. It does not prevent colds. It is of no value in treating frostbite. It does not relieve fatigue or shock. It does not enhance sexual performance—it may release inhibitions, but it impairs the follow-through. As a drug, its sedative value is offset by the toxic effect it has on the brain, heart, liver, and gastrointestinal tract. Medically speaking, there is no possible benefit which can be derived from the use of alcohol internally.

> "While consuming alcohol sensibly is associated with better health and longer life, the abuse of alcohol is associated with many undesirable health outcomes."

There Are Many Myths About the Harms of Alcohol Use

David J. Hanson

In the following viewpoint, David J. Hanson debunks several myths about drinking alcohol. He addresses numerous topics related to alcohol, including the alcohol content of various beverages, alcohol use among young people, and causes of alcoholism. Hanson is professor emeritus of sociology at the State University of New York, Potsdam. He maintains the Web site Alcohol: Problems & Solutions.

As you read, consider the following questions:

1. According to Hanson, is it true that switching among different kinds of alcoholic drinks will lead to intoxication more quickly?

2. What type of drinking is frequently mistakenly labeled as binge drinking, according to the author?

David J. Hanson, "Facts & Fiction," *Alcohol: Problems & Solutions*. www2.pots dam.edu/hansondj/AlcoholFactsAndFiction.html. Reproduced by permission.

3. Why would universal abstinence from alcohol not necessarily lead to a reduction in the loss of lives, according to Hanson?

This [viewpoint] corrects common alcohol and drinking myths, with research-based facts and statistics.

Myth: Alcohol destroys brain cells.

Fact: The moderate consumption of alcohol does not destroy brain cells. In fact it is often associated with improved cognitive (mental) functioning.

Myth: White wine is a good choice for a person who wants a light drink with less alcohol.

Fact: A glass of white or red wine, a bottle of beer, and a shot of whiskey or other distilled spirits all contain equivalent amounts of alcohol and are the same to a Breathalyzer. A standard drink is:

- A 12-ounce bottle or can of regular beer

- A 5-ounce glass of wine

- A one and 1/2 ounce [shot] of 80 proof distilled spirits (either straight or in a mixed drink)

Myth: A "beer belly" is caused by drinking beer.

Fact: A "beer belly" is caused by eating too much food. No beer or other alcohol beverage is necessary.

Myth: Switching between beer, wine and spirits will lead to intoxication more quickly than sticking to one type of alcohol beverage.

Fact: The level of blood alcohol content (BAC) is what determines sobriety or intoxication. Remember that a standard drink of beer, wine, or spirits contain equivalent amounts of alcohol. Alcohol is alcohol and a drink is a drink.

Myth: Drinking coffee will help a drunk person sober up.

Fact: Only time can sober up a person . . . not black coffee, cold showers, exercise, or any other common "cures." Alcohol leaves the body of virtually everyone at a constant rate of about .015 percent of blood alcohol content (BAC) per hour. Thus, a person with a BAC of .015 would be completely sober in an hour while a person with a BAC of ten times that (.15) would require 10 hours to become completely sober. This is true regardless of sex, age, weight, and similar factors.

Myth: Drinking long enough will cause a person to become alcoholic.

Fact: There is simply no scientific basis for this misperception, which appears to have its origin in temperance and prohibitionist ideology.

Myth: Drinking alcohol causes weight gain.

Fact: This is a very commonly believed myth, even among medical professionals, because alcohol has caloric value. However, extensive research around the world has found alcohol consumption does not cause weight gain in men and is often associated with a small weight loss in women.

Myth: Alcohol stunts the growth of children and retards their development.

Fact: Scientific medical research does not support this old temperance scare tactic promoted by the Women's Christian Temperance Union, the Anti-Saloon League, the Prohibition Party, and similar groups.

Myth: Binge drinking is an epidemic problem on college campuses.

Fact: Binge drinking is clinically and commonly viewed as a period of extended intoxication lasting at least several days during which time the binger drops out of usual life activities. Few university students engage in such bingeing behavior. However, a number sometimes consume at least four drinks in a day (or at least five for men). Although many of these young people may never even become intoxicated, they are branded as binge drinkers by some researchers. This practice deceptively inflates the number of apparent binge drinkers. In reality, the proportion of college students who drink continues to decline, as does the percentage of those who drink heavily.

Myth: Men and women of the same height and weight can drink the same.

Fact: Women are affected more rapidly because they tend to have a slightly higher proportion of fat to lean muscle tissue, thus concentrating alcohol a little more easily in their lower percentage of body water. They also have less of an enzyme (dehydrogenase) that metabolizes or breaks down alcohol, and hormonal changes during their menstrual cycle might also affect alcohol absorption to some degree.

Myth: A single sip of alcohol by a pregnant woman can cause her child to have fetal alcohol syndrome (FAS).

Fact: Extensive medical research studying hundreds of thousands of women from around the world fails to find scientific evidence that light drinking, much less a sip of alcohol by an expectant mother, can cause fetal alcohol syndrome. Of course, the very safest choice would be to abstain during the period of gestation.

Myth: People who abstain from alcohol are "alcohol-free."

Fact: Every person produces alcohol normally in the body 24 hours each and every day from birth until death. Therefore, we always have alcohol in our bodies.

Myth: Alcohol abuse is an increasing problem among young people.

Fact: Heavy alcohol use among people in the US 17 years of age or younger actually dropped by an amazing two-thirds (65.9 percent) between 1985 and 1997, according to federal government research. The proportion of young people who consumed any alcohol within the previous month dropped from 50% to 19% in about the same period. Other federally funded research also documents the continuing decline in both drinking and drinking abuse among young people. Similarly, alcohol-related traffic injuries and fatalities among young

Alcohol and Cognitive Functioning in Older Women

We found that older women who consumed up to one drink per day had consistently better cognitive performance than nondrinkers. Overall, as compared with nondrinkers, women who drank 1.0 to 14.9 g of alcohol per day had a decrease in the risk of cognitive impairment of about 20 percent. Moreover, moderate drinkers were less likely to have a substantial decline in cognitive function over a year period. We found similar inverse for all types of alcoholic beverages.

Schmidt, et. al., The New England Journal of Medicine, *2005.*

people continue to drop. Deaths associated with young drinking drivers aged 16 to 24 decreased almost half (47%) in a recent 15-year period.

Myth: People in the US are generally heavy consumers of alcohol.

Fact: The US isn't even among the top ten alcohol consuming countries. Top 10 Alcohol Consuming Countries on per capita Basis Country / Consumption in Gallons of absolute or pure alcohol: At a consumption rate of only 1.74 per person, the US falls far down at 32nd on the list.

Myth: The US has very lenient underage drinking laws.

Fact: The US has the most strict youth drinking laws in the Western world, including the highest minimum drinking age in the entire world. And this is buttressed by a public policy of *Zero Tolerance.*

Myth: Alcohol advertising increases drinking problems.

Fact: Hundreds of scientific research studies around the world have clearly demonstrated that alcohol advertising does not lead to increases in drinking abuse or drinking problems. Alcohol advertising continues because effective ads can increase a brand's share of the total market.

Myth: Bottles of tequila contain a worm.

Fact: There is no worm in tequila. It's in mescal, a spirit beverage distilled from a different plant. And it's not actually a worm, but a butterfly caterpillar (Hipopta Agavis) called a gurano.

Myth: People who can "hold their liquor" are to be envied.

Fact: People who can drink heavily without becoming intoxicated have probably developed a tolerance for alcohol, which can indicate the onset of dependency.

Myth: Many lives would be saved if everyone abstained from alcohol.

Fact: Some lives would be saved from accidents now caused by intoxication and from health problems caused by alcohol abuse. However, many other lives would be lost from increases in coronary heart disease. For example, estimates from 13 studies suggest that as many as 135,884 additional deaths would occur each year in the US from coronary heart disease alone because of abstinence.

Myth: Drunkenness and alcoholism are the same thing.

Fact: Many non-alcoholics on occasion become intoxicated or drunk. However, if they are not addicted to alcohol, they are not alcoholic. Of course, intoxication is never completely safe or risk-free and should be avoided. It is better either to abstain or to drink in moderation. While consuming alcohol sensibly is associated with better health and longer life, the abuse of alcohol is associated with many undesirable health outcomes.

Myth: Alcohol is the cause of alcoholism.

Fact: As a governmental alcohol agency has explained, "Alcohol no more causes alcoholism than sugar causes diabetes." The agency points out that if alcohol caused alcoholism then all drinkers would be alcoholics. In fact, a belief common among members of Alcoholics Anonymous (AA) is that people are born alcoholic and are not caused to be alcoholic by alcohol or anything in their experience. They argue that many people are born and die alcoholic without ever having had a sip of alcohol. Of course, a person can't be a drinking or practicing alcoholic without alcohol.

Myth: If alcohol were less available there would be fewer alcoholics.

Fact: This is an idea that has been tested through prohibition in the US and a number of other countries. There is no association between the availability of alcohol and alcoholism.

Myth: College life leads to drinking by most students who enter as abstainers.

Fact: According to Federal statistics, most students arrive at college with prior drinking experience and the proportion of drinkers doesn't increase greatly during college.

Myth: Although not totally incorrect, but certainly not the whole truth, is the assertion that the younger children are when they have their first drink the more likely they are to experience drinking problems.

Fact: Generally speaking, people who on their own begin drinking either much earlier or much later than their peers begin are more likely to experience subsequent drinking problems. This appears to result from the fact that either behavior tends to reflect a tendency to be deviant. Therefore, delaying the age of first drink would not influence the incidence of drinking problems because it would not change the underlying predisposition to be deviant and to experience drinking problems. And, of course, children who are taught moderation by their parents are less likely to abuse alcohol or have drinking problems.

| "*Tobacco use is the leading preventable cause of death in the United States.*"

Tobacco Use Is Addictive and Harmful

National Institute on Drug Abuse

In the following viewpoint, the National Institute on Drug Abuse (NIDA) argues that the nicotine in tobacco, consumed in cigarettes, cigars, and chewing tobacco, is extremely addictive and harmful. The authors explain the way the body absorbs and processes nicotine, and examine the medical consequences of using tobacco. NIDA is a part of the U.S. Department of Health & Human Services. NIDA supports and conducts research on drug abuse and addiction, with the goal of using the results to improve prevention, treatment, and policy.

As you read, consider the following questions:

1. According to the NIDA, what are nicotine's immediate effects on the body?

2. What are nicotine's withdrawal symptoms, according to the author?

3. What are some of the diseases linked to cigarette smoking, according to the National Institute on Drug Abuse?

National Institute on Drug Abuse, "National Institute on Drug Abuse Research Report—Tobacco Addiction," www.nida.nih.gov, July 2006.

According to the 2004 National Survey on Drug Use and Health, an estimated 70.3 million Americans age 12 or older reported current use of tobacco—59.9 million (24.9 percent of the population) were current cigarette smokers, 13.7 million (5.7 percent) smoked cigars, 1.8 million (0.8 percent) smoked pipes, and 7.2 million (3.0 percent) used smokeless tobacco, confirming that tobacco is one of the most widely abused substances in the United States. While these numbers are still unacceptably high, they represent a decrease of almost 50 percent since peak use in 1965.

NIDA's 2005 Monitoring the Future Survey of 8th-, 10th-, and 12th-graders, used to track drug use patterns and attitudes, has also shown a striking decrease in smoking trends among the Nation's youth. The latest results indicate that about 9 percent of 8th-graders, 15 percent of 10th-graders, and 23 percent of 12th-graders had used cigarettes in the 30 days prior to the survey. Despite cigarette use being at the lowest levels of the survey since a peak in the mid-1990s, the past few years indicate a clear slowing of this decline. And while perceived risk and disapproval of smoking had been on the rise, recent years have shown the rate of change to be dwindling. In fact, current use, perceived risk, and disapproval leveled off among 8th-graders in 2005, suggesting that renewed efforts are needed to ensure that teens understand the harmful consequences of smoking.

Moreover, the declining prevalence of cigarette smoking among the general U.S. population is not reflected in patients with mental illnesses. For them, it remains substantially higher, with the incidence of smoking in patients suffering from post-traumatic stress disorder, bipolar disorder, major depression, and other mental illness twofold to fourfold higher than the general population, and smoking incidence among people with schizophrenia as high as 90 percent.

Tobacco use is the leading preventable cause of death in the United States. The impact of tobacco use in terms of morbidity and mortality costs to society is staggering. Economically, more than $75 billion of total U.S. healthcare costs each year is attributable directly to smoking. However, this cost is well below the total cost to society because it does not include burn care from smoking-related fires, perinatal care for low birth-weight infants of mothers who smoke, and medical care costs associated with disease caused by secondhand smoke. In addition to healthcare costs, the costs of lost productivity due to smoking effects are estimated at $82 billion per year, bringing a conservative estimate of the economic burden of smoking to more than $150 billion per year.

The Effects of Nicotine

There are more than 4,000 chemicals found in the smoke of tobacco products. Of these, nicotine, first identified in the early 1800s, is the primary reinforcing component of tobacco that acts on the brain.

Cigarette smoking is the most popular method of using tobacco; however, there has also been a recent increase in the sale and consumption of smokeless tobacco products, such as snuff and chewing tobacco. These smokeless products also contain nicotine, as well as many toxic chemicals.

The cigarette is a very efficient and highly engineered drug-delivery system. By inhaling tobacco smoke, the average smoker takes in 1 to 2 mg of nicotine per cigarette. When tobacco is smoked, nicotine rapidly reaches peak levels in the bloodstream and enters the brain. A typical smoker will take 10 puffs on a cigarette over a period of 5 minutes that the cigarette is lit. Thus, a person who smokes about 1-1/2 packs (30 cigarettes) daily gets 300 "hits" of nicotine to the brain each day. In those who typically do not inhale the smoke—such as cigar and pipe smokers and smokeless tobacco users—nicotine is absorbed through the mucosal membranes and reaches peak blood levels and the brain more slowly.

Immediately after exposure to nicotine, there is a "kick" caused in part by the drug's stimulation of the adrenal glands and resulting discharge of epinephrine (adrenaline). The rush of adrenaline stimulates the body and causes a sudden release of glucose, as well as an increase in blood pressure, respiration, and heart rate. Nicotine also suppresses insulin output from the pancreas, which means that smokers are always slightly hyperglycemic (i.e., they have elevated blood sugar levels). The calming effect of nicotine reported by many users is usually associated with a decline in withdrawal effects rather than direct effects of nicotine.

Is Nicotine Addictive?

Yes. Most smokers use tobacco regularly because they are addicted to nicotine. Addiction is characterized by compulsive drug seeking and use, even in the face of negative health consequences. It is well documented that most smokers identify tobacco use as harmful and express a desire to reduce or stop using it, and nearly 35 million of them want to quit each year. Unfortunately, only about 6 percent of people who try to quit are successful for more than a month.

Research has shown how nicotine acts on the brain to produce a number of effects. Of primary importance to its addictive nature are findings that nicotine activates reward pathways—the brain circuitry that regulates feelings of pleasure. A key brain chemical involved in mediating the desire to consume drugs is the neurotransmitter dopamine, and research has shown that nicotine increases levels of dopamine in the reward circuits. This reaction is similar to that seen with other drugs of abuse, and is thought to underlie the pleasurable sensations experienced by many smokers. Nicotine's pharmacokinetic properties also enhance its abuse potential. Cigarette smoking produces a rapid distribution of nicotine to the brain, with drug levels peaking within 10 seconds of inhalation. However, the acute effects of nicotine dissipate in a few minutes, as do the associated feelings of reward, which causes the smoker to continue dosing to maintain the drug's pleasurable effects and prevent withdrawal.

Nicotine withdrawal symptoms include irritability, craving, cognitive and attentional deficits, sleep disturbances, and increased appetite. These symptoms may begin within a few hours after the last cigarette, quickly driving people back to tobacco use. Symptoms peak within the first few days of smoking cessation and may subside within a few weeks. For some people, however, symptoms may persist for months.

While withdrawal is related to the pharmacological effects of nicotine, many behavioral factors can also affect the severity of withdrawal symptoms. For some people, the feel, smell, and sight of a cigarette and the ritual of obtaining, handling, lighting, and smoking the cigarette are all associated with the pleasurable effects of smoking and can make withdrawal or craving worse. While nicotine gum and patches may alleviate the pharmacological aspects of withdrawal, cravings often persist. Other forms of nicotine replacement, such as inhalers, attempt to address some of these other issues, while behavioral therapies can help smokers identify environmental triggers of withdrawal and craving so they can employ strategies to prevent or circumvent these symptoms and urges.

Are There Other Chemicals That May Contribute to Tobacco Addiction?

Yes, research is showing that nicotine may not be the only psychoactive ingredient in tobacco. Using advanced neuro-imaging technology, scientists can see the dramatic effect of cigarette smoking on the brain and are finding a marked decrease in the levels of monoamine oxidase (MAO), an important enzyme that is responsible for the breakdown of dopamine. This change is likely caused by some tobacco smoke ingredient other than nicotine, since we know that nicotine itself does not dramatically alter MAO levels. The decrease in

Annual Deaths Attributable to Cigarette Smoking— United States, 1997–2001

About 438,000 U.S. Deaths Attributable Each Year to Cigarette Smoking*

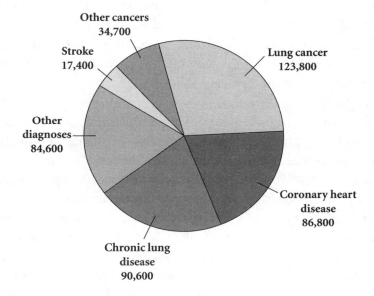

Other cancers
34,700

Stroke
17,400

Lung cancer
123,800

Other
diagnoses
84,600

Coronary heart
disease
86,800

Chronic lung
disease
90,600

*Average annual number of deaths, 1997–2001.

TAKEN FROM: Morbidity and Mortality Weekly Report (MMWR), Centers for Disease Control and Prevention, July 1, 2005.

two forms of MAO (A and B) results in higher dopamine levels and may be another reason that smokers continue to smoke—to sustain the high dopamine levels that lead to the desire for repeated drug use.

Recently, NIDA-funded researchers have shown in animals that acetaldehyde, another chemical constituent of tobacco smoke, dramatically increases the reinforcing properties of nicotine and may also contribute to tobacco addiction. The investigators further report that this effect is age-related, with adolescent animals displaying far more sensitivity to this reinforcing effect, suggesting that the brains of adolescents may be more vulnerable to tobacco addiction.

The Medical Consequences of Tobacco Use

Cigarette smoking kills an estimated 440,000 U.S. citizens each year—more than alcohol, cocaine, heroin, homicide, suicide, car accidents, fire, and AIDS combined. Since 1964, more than 12 million Americans have died prematurely from smoking, and another 25 million U.S. smokers alive today will most likely die of a smoking-related illness.

Cigarette smoking harms every organ in the body. It has been conclusively linked to leukemia, cataracts, and pneumonia, and accounts for about one-third of all cancer deaths. The overall rates of death from cancer are twice as high among smokers as nonsmokers, with heavy smokers having rates that are four times greater than those of nonsmokers. Foremost among the cancers caused by tobacco use is lung cancer—cigarette smoking has been linked to about 90 percent of all lung cancer cases, the number-one cancer killer of both men and women. Smoking is also associated with cancers of the mouth, pharynx, larynx, esophagus, stomach, pancreas, cervix, kidney, ureter, and bladder.

In addition to cancer, smoking causes lung diseases such as chronic bronchitis and emphysema, and it has been found to exacerbate asthma symptoms in adults and children. More than 90 percent of all deaths from chronic obstructive pulmonary diseases are attributable to cigarette smoking. It has also been well documented that smoking substantially increases the risk of heart disease, including stroke, heart attack, vascular disease, and aneurysm. It is estimated that smoking accounts for approximately 21 percent of deaths from coronary heart disease each year.

Exposure to high doses of nicotine, such as those found in some insecticide sprays, can be extremely toxic as well, causing vomiting, tremors, convulsions, and death. In fact, one drop of pure nicotine can kill a person. Nicotine poisoning has been reported from accidental ingestion of insecticides by adults and ingestion of tobacco products by children and pets. Death usually results in a few minutes from respiratory failure caused by paralysis.

While we often think of medical consequences that result from direct use of tobacco products, passive or secondary smoke also increases the risk for many diseases. Environmental tobacco smoke is a major source of indoor air contaminants; secondhand smoke is estimated to cause approximately 3,000 lung cancer deaths per year among nonsmokers and contributes to more than 35,000 deaths related to cardiovascular disease. Exposure to tobacco smoke in the home is also a risk factor for new cases and increased severity of childhood asthma and has been associated with sudden infant death syndrome. Additionally, dropped cigarettes are the leading cause of residential fire fatalities, leading to more than 1,000 deaths each year.

Are There Safe Tobacco Products?

The adverse health effects of tobacco use are well known, yet many people do not want to quit or have difficulty quitting. As a result, there has been a recent surge in the development of tobacco products that claim to reduce exposure to harmful tobacco constituents or to have fewer health risks than conventional products. These "potentially reduced exposure products" (or PREPs), which include cigarettes and smokeless tobacco (e.g., snuff, tobacco lozenges), have not yet been evaluated sufficiently to determine whether they are indeed associated with reduced risk of disease. Recent studies indicate that the levels of carcinogens in these PREPs range from relatively low to comparable to conventional tobacco products. These studies conclude that medicinal nicotine (found in the nicotine patch and gum) is a safer alternative than these modified tobacco products.

The Risks of Smoking and Pregnancy

In the United States, it is estimated that 18 percent of pregnant women smoke during their pregnancies. Carbon monoxide and nicotine from tobacco smoke may interfere with the oxygen supply to the fetus. Nicotine also readily crosses the placenta, with concentrations in the fetus reaching as much as 15 percent higher than maternal levels. Nicotine concentrates in fetal blood, amniotic fluid, and breast milk. Combined, these factors can have severe consequences for the fetuses and infants of smoking mothers. Smoking during pregnancy caused an estimated 910 infant deaths annually from 1997 through 2001, and neonatal care costs related to smoking are estimated to be more than $350 million per year.

The adverse effects of smoking during pregnancy can include fetal growth retardation and decreased birth weights. The decreased birth weights seen in infants of mothers who smoke reflect a dose-dependent relationship—the more the woman smokes during pregnancy, the greater the reduction of infant birth weight. These newborns also display signs of stress and drug withdrawal consistent with what has been reported in infants exposed to other drugs. In some cases, smoking during pregnancy may be associated with spontaneous abortions, sudden infant death syndrome, as well as learning and behavioral problems in children. In addition, smoking more than a pack a day during pregnancy nearly doubles the risk that the affected child will become addicted to tobacco if that child starts smoking. . . .

Smoking and Adolescence

There are nearly 4 million American adolescents who have used a tobacco product in the past month [June 2006]. Nearly 90 percent of smokers start smoking by age 18, and of smokers under 18 years of age, more than 6 million will die prematurely from a smoking-related disease.

Tobacco use in teens is not only the result of psychosocial influences, such as peer pressure; recent research suggests that there may be biological reasons for this period of increased vulnerability. Indeed, even intermittent smoking can result in the development of tobacco addiction in some teens. Animal models of teen smoking provide additional evidence of an increased vulnerability. Adolescent rats are more susceptible to the reinforcing effects of nicotine than adult rats, and take more nicotine when it is available than do adult animals.

Adolescents may also be more sensitive to the reinforcing effects of nicotine in combination with other chemicals found in cigarettes, thus increasing susceptibility to tobacco addiction. As mentioned above, acetaldehyde increases nicotine's addictive properties in adolescent, but not adult, animals. That is, adolescent animals performing a task to receive nicotine showed greater response rates to nicotine when combined with acetaldehyde. NIDA continues to actively support research aimed at increasing our understanding of why and how adolescents become addicted, and to develop prevention, intervention, and treatment strategies to meet the specific needs of teens.

| "It has become fashionable to blame smoking for just about anything."

Harms from Tobacco Use Are Overstated and Distorted

Joe Jackson

In the following viewpoint, Joe Jackson argues that the risks of smoking have been overstated. Focusing on the risk of cancer, he argues that statistics have been distorted to make smoking seem like a greater risk than it is in actuality. Additionally, Jackson disputes the argument for the addictiveness of nicotine, pointing to the number of casual smokers and arguing against the notion of addiction, more generally. Joe Jackson is a musician who has been publicly outspoken against antismoking hysteria and smoking bans.

As you read, consider the following questions:

1. What does Jackson mean when he says that lung cancer and smoking are statistically related, rather than causally related?

2. Why are the statistics regarding deaths from "smoking-related diseases" misleading, according to the author?

Joe Jackson, *Smoke, Lies and the Nanny State*, www.joejackson.com, April 2007. Reproduced by permission.

3. Why does the author claim that "addiction" is not a clearly defined scientific term?

Smoking has always been something which many people love and many others just don't get. As far as they're concerned, it quite literally stinks. They therefore tend to believe any horror story they hear about it. . .

Lung Cancer, and Convenient Numbers

We seem to be obsessed with cancer these days, perhaps because the idea that something is still beyond the power of doctors and scientists scares the living daylights out of us. I don't mean to trivialise; my father died of cancer. I do think, though, that we're overly zealous in our search for scapegoats (recent media reports have claimed that we can get cancer from hair dye, soft drinks and oral sex). I also want to point out—turning the negative into a positive for once—that cancer is mostly a disease of the old, and another reason it looms so large is that we're living longer and mostly healthier lives than at any time in history.

Lung cancer is the disease most strongly associated with smoking, though even this is a statistical rather than a causative link. In other words, it has been statistically shown that smokers are more likely to get lung cancer, rather than scientifically shown that the cancer is specifically caused by the smoking. This is a more important distinction than it might seem. Much of the antismokers' case is based on statistics, and statistics is not science.

It does make sense—so long as you don't mind bullying people out of their pleasures—to try to bring down the rate of lung cancer by getting people to quit smoking. But the evidence linking smoking with lung cancer is much less convincing than we are led to believe. For one thing, there is much disagreement about what the actual risk factor is.

The general consensus seems to reflect the pioneering studies of Professor Sir Richard Doll in the 1950s and 60s, which are still regarded as 'benchmarks'. Doll reckoned that about 160 in 100,000 smokers developed lung cancer as opposed to 7 in 100,000 nonsmokers; so you have about a 24 times greater risk if you smoke. This can also be expressed as '2,400%'. But beware of estimates of 'increased risk,' especially when expressed in percentages; they're a good sign that someone is trying to frighten, rather than to inform.

If you buy 25 lottery tickets instead of one, your chances of winning go up by 2,500%. But though the number sounds impressive, your actual chances of winning are still minuscule.

Likewise, if Prof Doll was right, you still have a 99.8% chance of not getting lung cancer. This is nothing more or less than a re-presentation, or re-packaging, of the same data. But it immediately sounds a lot less scary. Especially if smoking is something you love.

More Inconvenient Numbers

Statistics always present one version of reality while leaving out many others. For instance: antismokers' increased-risk estimates leave out the fact that a majority of lung cancers happen within, or beyond, the normal range of death. In other words, if lung cancer is going to get you, it'll probably do so around the time when *something* is going to get you, whether you smoke or not.

There are also many contradictory statistics out there for those who care to look. Native Americans have half the rate of lung cancer of white Americans even though they smoke much more. Very few Chinese women smoke and yet they have one of the highest lung cancer rates in the world. Lung cancer rates practically everywhere have been rising since about 1930 and in some cases (e.g. American women) have not peaked yet, despite the fact that smoking rates have gone steadily down. Japan, one of the world's heaviest-smoking nations, is also in the top two or three in life expectancy. Japanese rates of lung cancer and heart disease have nevertheless been rising for the last 3 decades—at the same time as their smoking rate has gone down. Perhaps this is because their diet and lifestyle have become increasingly Americanised. I really don't know. All I'm saying is that 'inconvenient' facts should be investigated, rather than swept under the carpet.

The more you look into this sort of thing, the murkier it gets. Even the term 'smoker' is defined differently in different studies; some only look at heavy long-term cigarette smokers (there is very little risk in cigar or pipe smoking anyway) but others define anyone who has smoked 100 cigarettes in their life as a 'smoker,' others count as smokers people who quit 20 years before, and so on.

Antismokers maintain that smoking is responsible for about 90% of lung cancer deaths. But the Lung Cancer Alliance, a US lobby group, maintains that a half of lung cancer victims have never smoked.

All cancers have multiple risk factors (about 40 have been identified for lung cancer) and no one really knows why some people get sick and others don't. Lung cancer is the easiest disease to link with smoking, but even in this case, the danger cannot possibly be anywhere near as great as we're currently being told. Of course, many people have given up since the US Surgeon General's announcement in 1964, that smoking could cause lung cancer. But no matter how many people quit, it's never enough for the antismoking zealots. This is why they've turned their attention more and more to:

The Smoking-Related Disease

This is one of the antismokers' cleverest inventions. To say that a disease is 'smoking-related' is *not* the same as saying that it is directly caused by smoking, or that there is any actual proof of anything. It means simply that someone has decided that smoking *may be a factor* in that disease.

Over the last couple of decades, more and more diseases have been added to the list, often with very little evidence.

Smoking Risks

In a free and open society people must be allowed to operate as free agents without the fetters of the doomsayers. Life is a risk, but it is that risk which gives it zest. When we allow ourselves to sacrifice our freedoms for the sake of safety, we deserve neither safety nor freedom. Accepting statistics at face value will lead us down that garden path. There are many statistics that can be cited that make the danger of smoking seem mild by comparison.

For example, the use of cell phones, hair dryers, and electric blankets have higher risks than SHS [Second Hand Smoke]. About half of the smoking population has quit over the past 30 years, yet there has been no comparable increase in life expectancy. The smoke haters will quickly tell you this is because of the effects of second-hand smoke. The fallacy of their argument is that if there has been smoking there has also been second-hand smoke. In spite of the decline of smoking, childhood illnesses such as asthma, ear infections and A.D.D are rapidly increasing. Cigarettes and/or smoke have about 4,000 identifiable chemicals. Your daily diet has about 10,000 such chemicals. Arsenic which is considered a leading cause of lung cancer is found in significantly larger quantities in a glass of water than in a cigarette.

Robert Hayes Halfpenny,
The Smokers Club, Inc., 2005.

Heart disease was one of the first, even though it has something like 300 risk factors, and some major studies (for instance, that of the citizens of Framingham, Massachusetts, which has been going on since 1948) have shown not only that the link with smoking is weak, but that moderate smokers have less heart disease than nonsmokers.

More recently it has become fashionable to blame smoking for just about everything, from 'clogging up' of the arteries (which happens to everyone as they get older) to blindness (well, they can't blame masturbation any more) to AIDS. It has also become fashionable, every time a smoker dies, to try to find a way to blame their death on smoking.

Recent media scares have claimed that smoking 'may' cause impotence or infertility. But people smoked more during the two world wars than at any other time in history, and what did we have in the 1950s? A baby boom! Other scares have found their way onto cigarette packets. 'Smoking causes ageing of the skin' says one. Well, maybe, for some people, but there are clearly more important factors. Like the sun. And ageing.

The fact is that many statistics about smoking (and especially 'secondhand' smoke) are simply made up. For instance, until cervical cancer was recently proven to be caused by a virus, a completely random 13% of cases were attributed to smoking. Many of the estimates of smoking deaths are produced by one computer program. It's called SAMMEC (Smoking Attributable Morbidity, Mortality, and Economic Cost) and depending on which data you feed in, and which you leave out, it can produce pretty much any number you want.

The great thing about the 'smoking-related disease', is that it allows you to create the perception of a raging epidemic. The UK government says that 100,000 or 120,000 deaths per year (depending on who is speaking at the time) are caused by 'smoking-related disease'. The impression given is that these are all deaths specifically, and provably, caused by smoking, but it is no such thing. It includes nonsmokers who die of bronchitis or strokes, and smokers who die of heart attacks in their 80s. It includes people who quit smoking decades before. It is not exactly lying, but it is deliberately misleading, it is fearmongering, and in my opinion these people should be ashamed of themselves.

The Dose Makes the Poison

This is an old, but often ignored, scientific axiom. What it means is that there are safe and unsafe levels of *everything*. A little bit of arsenic is just fine. A significantly large amount of orange juice could kill you. But antismokers are now trying to sell us a scientific absurdity: that smoking is dangerous at *any level*.

It would seem obvious that there's a big difference between smoking five a day and fifty a day. Heaven forbid, though, that we should use our own common sense. In fact there is a great deal of evidence that moderate smoking—up to about ten a day—is not harmful, and indeed has clear benefits. Apart from pleasure (which current medical thinking deems irrelevant) it relieves stress, helps with weight control, and protects against or relieves the symptoms of quite a few diseases, including Alzheimer's, Parkinson's, ulcerative colitis, and cancers of the intestines and womb. Several doctors have admitted this to me in private, but you won't hear it from the medical institutions and lobby groups who have worked so hard to build smoking into Public Health Enemy No 1.

A couple of years ago I had the pleasure of meeting with the late Dr Ken Denson, head of the Thame Thrombosis and Haemostasis Research Centre in Oxfordshire, who was a rare and inspiring objector to what he called the antismoking 'witch hunt'. Dr Denson had devoted ten years to researching smoking, and published several medical journal articles eloquently arguing that the evidence, if looked at impartially and *in total*, was equivocal. He had unearthed countless studies showing that changes in diet could offset any risks, that moderate smokers who exercised had less disease than nonsmokers, and so on, and simply wanted to know why such studies were ignored while anything appearing to show the slightest risk was trumpeted from the rooftops. In Dr Denson's view, doctors were failing smokers by preaching zero-tolerance instead of balance and moderation. He also suggested that we talk about 'smokers-related', rather than 'smoking-related' diseases, since a majority of smokers have tended to have overall unhealthy lifestyles.

In Britain we're now being told that the working class and poor have much more disease than the middle class, and the main reason is smoking. But poorer and less-educated people are more likely to get poor health care, have bad diets, drink too much, work too hard, exercise too little, be more affected by stress and pollution, etc etc . . . all factors in 'smoking-related' disease which are impossible to separate from smoking itself. You can always single out something as the Curse of the Working Classes. In 1920s America it was booze; now it's tobacco.

P.A.S. (Pathetic Addict Syndrome)

Antismokers tell us that people only smoke because they are 'addicted to nicotine', and that most smokers actually want to quit. But most smokers enjoy smoking, and few people *want* to quit something they enjoy. Nag and frighten them enough, though, and you can certainly get them to believe that they *should*.

'Addiction' not a clearly-defined scientific term, and it's very hard to separate 'addictions' from habits, rituals, or pleasures that we constantly repeat because they are, well, pleasurable. Probably everyone is 'addicted' to something: alcohol, sugar, caffeine, drugs both legal and illegal, sex, television, dieting, gambling, shopping, computer games, football, cars, or the gym. Of course, I recognise that some people find it hard to be moderate. But I think this is a question of personality, or perhaps genetic predisposition, rather than the 'fault' of the substance in question—or whoever sold it to you.

The Elizabethans who were the first European smokers observed that tobacco could become a habit which some found very hard to break. But, as Iain Gately points out in his excellent history of tobacco, *La Diva Nicotine*, they would have been baffled by our concept of 'addiction', since they believed that all human beings were granted by God the gift of free will. The idea that a man could be enslaved by a plant would have seemed to them absurd. I must confess this view makes more sense to me than the fashionable contemporary one which sees helpless victims everywhere, all needing to be protected either from themselves or from evil forces such as tobacco companies—who, conveniently, can then be sued for large sums of money.

Nicotine is not harmful. It is a naturally occurring substance present not only in tobacco but, for instance, tomatoes. The potentially harmful ingredients in a cigarette are tar and carbon monoxide created by combustion, along with various other common carcinogens and poisons at infinitesimal levels. (Note to you ex-hippies who've jumped on the anti-tobacco bandwagon: this is also true of other smokeables). Anyway, if nicotine is dangerous, why on earth are doctors trying so hard to sell it to us in the form of patches, gums and inhalers?

Antismokers have to keep pushing 'addiction' since they either cannot believe, or cannot admit, that people not only freely choose to smoke but enjoy it. 'Addiction' also works to further stigmatise smokers by portraying us as contemptible junkies. Of course, if you're smoking out of pure compulsion and aren't even enjoying it, I would say you might as well quit. After all, if you're going to do something which not only has potential health risks but increasingly gets you treated like dirt, then you may as well at least get some pleasure from it. But many thousands have quit of their own accord, and many others are smoking moderately, or only at certain times. or switching to cigars. I meet these people all the time, but according to antismokers they don't exist. I personally only smoke when I'm having a drink. Perhaps I don't exist either.

Periodical Bibliography

The following articles have been selected to supplement the diverse views presented in this chapter.

George W. Dowdall "The Functions and Dysfunctions of Youth Alcohol Use," *Nutrition Today*, January–February 2003.

Rutger C. M. E. Engels "Beneficial Functions of Alcohol Use in Adolescents: Theory and Implications for Prevention," *Nutrition Today*, January—February 2003.

The Independent "So How Dangerous is Cannabis?" June 28, 2006.

Scott Jaschik "An Honest Conversation about Alcohol," *Inside Higher Ed*, February 16, 2007.

Kathiann M. Kowalski "Alcohol: A Real Threat," *Current Health 2: A Weekly Reader*, December 2003.

Jacqueline W. Miller et al. "Binge Drinking and Associated Health Risk Behaviors Among High School Students," *Pediatrics*, January 2007.

National Institute on Drug Abuse (NIDA) "Cigarettes and Other Tobacco Products," *NIDA InfoFacts*, July 2006.

Office of National Drug Control Policy (ONDCP) "What Americans Need to Know About Marijuana: Important Facts About Our Nation's Most Misunderstood Illegal Drug," October 2003.

Sandy Fertman Ryan "Wasted Lives: The Truth about Teen Girls and Drinking," *Girls' Life*, October–November 2004.

Pamela Sherrid "Smokers' Revenge," *U.S. News & World Report*, November 4, 2002.

OPPOSING
VIEWPOINTS®
SERIES

CHAPTER 3

What Is the Relationship Between Gateway Drugs and Other Drugs?

Chapter Preface

Tobacco, alcohol, and marijuana are the most common drugs to be charged as having a gateway effect, but they are not the only ones. Recently, caffeine has come under fire for being a gateway drug to other substances. A study by the National Center on Addiction and Substance Abuse at Columbia University (CASA) in 2003 titled *The Formative Years: Pathways to Substance Abuse among Girls and Young Women Ages 8–22*, finds that "young women who drink coffee began smoking cigarettes and using alcohol at an earlier age and use more of these substances than girls and young women who do not drink coffee." CASA includes "frequent coffee drinking" on a list of warning signs for substance abuse among young girls and young women.

In 2005, ABC News reported that there was concern over a new product, KickStart SPARK, an energy drink being marketed to children. Spark contains 60 milligrams of caffeine—a little more than half of the amount of caffeine found in a typical cup of coffee—as well as vitamins. Concern about the link between caffeine consumption in kids and later drug use was expressed by a doctor quoted in the news story who stated, "Recommending that children and adolescents use Spark may be a slippery slope toward the use of other performance-enhancing products, or even the abuse of illicit substances." The concern is that since caffeine is a stimulating drug that many people rely on to stay alert, people who use that drug may be more likely to use other drugs for other needs or desires.

Many reject the claim that caffeine should be considered a gateway drug. Jacob Sullum denies that there is any effect of caffeine that would cause people to use other drugs. Assuming a correlation between caffeine use and later use of tobacco or alcohol, as cited in the CASA study, Sullum argues that there is a simpler explanation for the correlation: "People who like caffeine, for instance, are more apt than people who don't to like other stimulants, such as nicotine." The correlation between drinking coffee and smoking cigarettes has an alternate explanation besides that of positing a gateway effect of coffee.

In response to the ABC News story, R. Warren Anderson notes, "If caffeine were a gateway drug, then this nation would be in peril. The average American consumes 1.64 cups of coffee per day." Because of the widespread use of caffeine, Anderson believes that if coffee had a gateway effect causing use of other drugs, widespread drug use other than coffee would be apparent. Anderson implies that he does not think there is evidence of this.

In the following chapter, the authors debate whether or not tobacco, alcohol, or marijuana should be considered gateway drugs. They each consider evidence and draw conclusions based on the evidence regarding a gateway effect.

| "Teens who smoke cigarettes are 14 times likelier than those who do not to try marijuana."

Cigarette Smoking Among Teens Is a Gateway to Marijuana Use

The National Center on Addiction and Substance Abuse at Columbia University

In the following viewpoint, the National Center on Addiction and Substance Abuse at Columbia University (CASA) argues that there is a correlation between teen cigarette smoking and teen marijuana use. In particular, CASA claims that teens who smoke cigarettes are much more likely to use marijuana than teens who do not smoke. The National Center on Addiction and Substance Abuse at Columbia University (CASA) is a nonprofit organization that aims to inform Americans of the economic and social costs of substance abuse.

As you read, consider the following questions:

1. According to the author, among teens who try marijuana, what percentages smoked cigarettes first, did not smoke cigarettes first, and smoked cigarettes at about the same time as trying marijuana?

The National Center on Addiction and Substance Abuse at Columbia University (CASA), *Report on Teen Cigarette Smoking and Marijuana Use*, 2003. www.casa columbia.org. Copyright © 2003. All rights reserved. Reproduced by permission.

2. According to CASA, what are the percentages of teens that can buy marijuana in an hour or less among teens who have never smoked, teens who have tried cigarettes, and teens who currently smoke cigarettes?

3. How much likelier are drugs to be used at schools where smoking occurs than at schools where smoking is not tolerated, according to the author?

For eight years, CASA has been engaged in the unprecedented undertaking of surveying attitudes of teens and those who most influence them—parents, teachers and school principals. While other surveys seek to measure the extent of substance abuse in the population, the *CASA National Survey of American Attitudes on Substance Abuse VIII: Teens and Parents* probes substance-abuse risk and identities factors that increase or diminish the likelihood that teens will abuse tobacco, alcohol or illegal drugs. We regard this effort as a work in progress and strive to refine it each year.

This year, for the first time, working with the American Legacy Foundation, CASA asked a series of questions to examine statistical associations between teen cigarette smoking and teen marijuana use.

The troubling findings:

- Teens who smoke cigarettes are 14 times likelier than those who do not to try marijuana.

- Among teens who admit to having tried marijuana, those who do not smoke cigarettes are likelier to have tried marijuana only once.

- Teens who have tried marijuana and are current cigarette smokers are 60 percent likelier to be repeat (as opposed to one-time) marijuana users.

- Teens who are current cigarette smokers are six limes likelier than those who have never smoked cigarettes to report that they can buy marijuana in an hour or less.

- Fifty-five percent of teens who are current cigarette smokers report more than half their friends use marijuana, compared with only three percent of those who have never smoked cigarettes.

- Among teens who are repeat marijuana users, 60 percent tried cigarettes first.

- Seventy-seven percent of teens believe that a teen who smokes cigarettes is more likely to use marijuana.

Cigarette Smoking and Marijuana

A teen who is a current smoker (i.e., one who smoked within the past 30 days) is 14 times likelier to try marijuana than a teen who has never smoked cigarettes (84 percent vs. six percent). A teen who is a current smoker is almost twice as likely to try marijuana than a teen who has tried cigarettes but is not a current smoker (84 percent vs. 45 percent).

Of teens who have tried marijuana once, 20 percent are current cigarette smokers. Of teens who are repeat marijuana users, 43 percent are current cigarette smokers.

Among teens who have tried marijuana:

- 57 percent smoked cigarettes first;

- 29 percent have not smoked cigarettes;

- 13 percent smoked cigarettes at about the same time or after they tried marijuana.

Thus, a 50 percent reduction in teen cigarette smoking could affect a substantial reduction in teen marijuana use—as much as 16.5 percent to 28.5 percent. The high end of the range assumes that half of the 57 percent of teens who smoked cigarettes first would not have smoked marijuana if they had not smoked cigarettes. The low end assumes that 42 percent of the 57 percent of teens who smoked cigarettes first might use marijuana even if they had not smoked cigarettes first.

Repeat Marijuana Use More Common Among Teens Who Smoke Cigarettes

Among teens who have tried marijuana, some have tried marijuana only once and others are repeat marijuana users. Whether a teen is a one-time user or a repeat user of marijuana is associated with the teen's cigarette smoking experience.

Among those teens who have tried marijuana and are current cigarette smokers, 62 percent are repeat marijuana users and 38 percent used marijuana only once. The results flip when the teens are not current smokers: Among teens who have tried marijuana and have also tried cigarettes but are not current cigarette smokers, 38 percent are repeat marijuana users and 60 percent used marijuana only once. Among teens who have tried marijuana but have never smoked cigarettes, 31 percent are repeat marijuana users and 67 percent used marijuana only once.

Teens who are repeat marijuana users are likely to have started by smoking nicotine cigarettes: Among teens who are repeat marijuana users, 60 percent tried cigarettes first.

Availability of Marijuana

Marijuana is a pervasive presence for those teens who smoke cigarettes. Seventy-six percent of those teens who are current cigarette smokers can buy marijuana in an hour or less. Thirty-six percent of those teens who have tried cigarettes but are not current smokers can buy marijuana in an hour or less. Thirteen percent of teens who have never smoked cigarettes can buy marijuana in an hour or less.

Teen current cigarette smokers are more likely than teen non-smokers to report that most of their friends use marijuana. Fifty-five percent of teen smokers report that more than half of their friends use marijuana, compared with 15 percent of those teens who have tried cigarettes but are not current smokers and three percent of those teens who have never smoked.

Teen Perceptions About Cigarette Smoking and Marijuana Use

Teens perceive a connection between cigarette smoking and marijuana use: When asked whether they think that a teen who smokes cigarettes is more likely to use marijuana, 77 percent respond in the affirmative.

Drugs in Schools

In schools where smoking occurs, 36 percent are drug free (i.e., schools where drugs are not used, kept or sold) and 62 percent are not drug free. In schools where smoking cigarettes on school grounds is not tolerated, 73 percent are drug free and 26 percent are not.

| "Craving for nicotine appears to increase craving for illicit drugs among drug abusers who also smoke tobacco."

Tobacco Use Is Linked to Cocaine and Heroin Use

Patrick Zickler

In the following viewpoint, Patrick Zickler argues that recent research shows a correlation between nicotine craving and cravings for illicit drugs, such as cocaine and heroin, among drug abusers. Zickler also claims that the research shows a correlation between the levels of tobacco use and levels of illicit drug use among drug users. Patrick Zickler is a staff writer for NIDA Notes, *a publication of the National Institute on Drug Abuse, a part of the U.S. Department of Health & Human Services.*

As you read, consider the following questions:

1. Who participated in the NIDA study at the Intramural Research Program that looked at the interaction between nicotine cravings and illicit drug cravings?

2. What happened to the participants in the study when exposed to tobacco craving messages, according to the author?

Patrick Zickler, "Nicotine Craving and Heavy Smoking May Contribute to Increased Use of Cocaine and Heroin," *NIDA Notes*, vol. 15, October 2000. www.nida.nih.gov.

3. Who participated in the NIDA study at the University of California that looked at the connection between tobacco smoking and illicit drug use?

People who abuse drugs are also likely to be cigarette smokers. More than two-thirds of drug abusers are regular tobacco smokers, a rate more than double that of the rest of the population. NIDA researchers have found that craving for nicotine appears to increase craving for illicit drugs among drug abusers who also smoke tobacco, and this relationship suggests that smokers in drug treatment programs may be less successful than nonsmokers in staying off drugs.

The Correlation of Cravings

At NIDA's Intramural Research Program in Baltimore, Dr. Stephen Heishman and his colleagues examined the interaction of craving for nicotine and craving for other drugs and found that situations that increased desire to smoke also increased desire to use drugs. The study involved male and female adult smokers who were not trying to stop smoking and had histories of abusing alcohol, cocaine, heroin, marijuana, and/or other substances.

The researchers asked participants to listen to recorded scripts describing scenes and then to rate their urge to smoke and their desire to use other drugs. In the first part of the study, which involved 18 participants, the scripts had content that was generally pleasant (watching children on a sunny beach), unpleasant (a friend asking to borrow money), or neutral (doing household chores). Some scripts also included people expressing a desire to smoke, while others did not mention smoking at all. Both the scripts including a mention of smoking and those containing negative emotional content increased the participants' craving for drugs, as well as for smoking.

In the second part of the study, 24 participants heard scripts with only pleasant content (enjoying the beach, talking

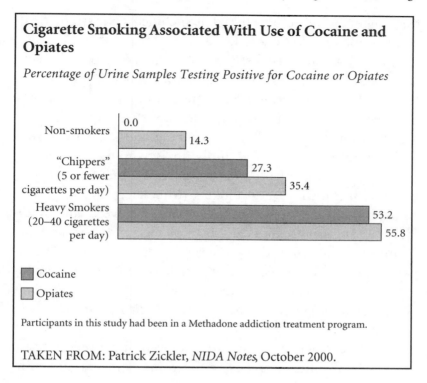

Cigarette Smoking Associated With Use of Cocaine and Opiates

Percentage of Urine Samples Testing Positive for Cocaine or Opiates

Non-smokers: 0.0 / 14.3

"Chippers" (5 or fewer cigarettes per day): 27.3 / 35.4

Heavy Smokers (20–40 cigarettes per day): 53.2 / 55.8

■ Cocaine
□ Opiates

Participants in this study had been in a Methadone addiction treatment program.

TAKEN FROM: Patrick Zickler, *NIDA Notes,* October 2000.

on the phone with an old acquaintance, or visiting friends). These scripts also contained descriptions of tobacco craving that increased in intensity from no mention of smoking to asking the question, "How could you really enjoy yourself fully unless you were smoking?" Participants reported that craving for both drugs and tobacco increased as the intensity of the tobacco craving messages in the scripts increased.

What This Means for Treatment

"One of our more interesting findings was that scripts that elicited craving for tobacco also elicited craving for the subject's drug of choice. This suggests that real-world situations that produce tobacco craving also may result in craving for drugs of abuse," Dr. Heishman says. The findings also suggest that treatment for heroin, cocaine, or alcohol addiction might be more effective if it included concurrent treatment of tobacco addiction, he says.

In a NIDA-supported study at the University of California, San Diego, doctoral candidate Dominick Frosch and his colleagues at the Integrated Substance Abuse Program at the University of California, Los Angeles, investigated the relationship between levels of cigarette smoking and levels of cocaine and heroin use among 32 individuals who had been in a methadone treatment program for at least 4 months. The participants included 10 nonsmokers (6 female, 4 male) and 22 smokers (16 female, 6 male). The smokers were equally divided among heavy smokers (20 to 40 cigarettes per day) and "chippers" who smoked 5 or fewer cigarettes per day. "Compared with heavy smokers, chippers have less intense craving for their first cigarette of the day and can more comfortably avoid smoking in situations where it is not permitted," Mr. Frosch explains.

The researchers evaluated the connection between tobacco smoking and illicit drug use among the smokers and nonsmokers by using breath and urine samples from the participants over a 7-day period. They found that the amount of cocaine and heroin use was closely related to the level of tobacco use. "The more cigarettes smoked, the more likely the person was to use illegal drugs," Mr. Frosch says. "These findings provide compelling reasons for implementing smoking cessation programs for patients in methadone treatment, as the benefits of smoking cessation may extend to opiate addiction as well."

"*The more alcohol someone drinks the more likely they will be to want to smoke marijuana.*"

Alcohol Use Is a Gateway to Marijuana Use

Alyssa J. Myers and Marion O. Petty

In the following viewpoint, Alyssa J. Myers and Marion O. Petty hypothesize that while marijuana is more often labeled a gateway drug, alcohol also poses a threat in terms of leading to other drug use. Myers and Petty describe a study they conducted that tests this hypothesis, and they argue that the results show that the more alcohol people drink, the more likely they are to smoke marijuana. Alyssa J. Myers and Marion O. Petty conducted this study while students at Missouri Western State University.

As you read, consider the following questions:

1. What drugs do the authors hypothesize as the biggest gateway drugs?
2. What distinguished the three groups observed in the experiment?

Alyssa J. Myers and Marion O. Petty, "Is Alcohol a Gateway Drug?" National Undergraduate Research Clearinghouse, Missouri Western State University, May 4, 2004. http://clearinghouse.missouriwestern.edu/manuscripts/481.asp. Reproduced by permission.

3. What were the different experiment results among the three groups, as reported by the authors?

Illegal drug use is a major issue in the United States. Every-day we are bombarded with anti-drug commercials, with marijuana use being the main target. It is taught from an early age that drug usage is negative and carries disastrous consequences. The problem with this, however, is that alcohol use is more common and even encouraged through advertising mediums such as commercials and billboards. Rather than teaching youths lifelong abstinence, they are in effect being encouraged to indulge when they are of legal age. The age is even lower for tobacco use, as adults as young as 18 in most states are of legal age to purchase tobacco.

According to the 2002 *Time Almanac* currently 51.7% of people use alcohol and only 5% of people are current marijuana users. Of the 51.7% of people that use alcohol 7.4% are heavy users. A study by the National Institute on Drug Abuse (NIDA) and the National Institute on Alcohol Abuse and Alcoholism (NIAAA) says the cost of alcohol and abuse was $246 billion in 1992, and that 60% or $148 billion of that was generated from alcoholism and alcohol abuse. More money is spent on alcohol abusers than on drug abusers every year. This implies that alcohol abuse is a bigger problem then marijuana use.

The Problem with Legal Drugs

Alcohol and tobacco are common drugs that can be found anywhere and used by anyone. The availability of these drugs makes [them] easier for kids to get and abuse at a young age. Studies have found that alcohol and tobacco abuse may lead to other illegal drug use.

Australian teenagers, aged 13 to 17 years were surveyed in a study done by Debra Blaze-Temple and Sing Kai Lo in 1992. They found that drug use increased with age. They also found that alcohol and tobacco were important "gateway" drugs and led to increased use of illegal drugs. Blaze-Temple and Kai Lo also state "Marijuana use was not a necessary stage for the progression to other illicit dug use as 29% of current users of other illicit drugs reported never using marijuana".

A study done by Shillington and Clapp in 2002 found that substance abuse and behavioral problems were higher among persons using both alcohol and marijuana then among those who used only alcohol or marijuana. Youth with alcohol problems also tend to be binge drinkers. Binge drinkers are "significantly more likely to report 'ever' using and current use of cigarettes, marijuana, cocaine, and other illegal drug." The more often binge drinking occurs the more likely people are to report use of cigarettes, marijuana, cocaine, and other illegal drugs.

Alcohol has been linked to criminal behavior. Research with convicted prisoners has suggested that many of them performed a lot of their crimes under the influence of alcohol. Day reported that 38% of the Canadian federal prison inmates committed their most serious crime while under the influence of alcohol.

Common knowledge suggests that marijuana is one of the worst drugs available. And experimentation with other illegal drugs stems from the initial use of marijuana. This is just not true. Use of illegal drugs also takes place after experimenting with two of the most common legal drugs available: alcohol and tobacco. After speaking with many individuals it has become clear that the majority of people do not realize that alcohol and tobacco are two of the biggest gateway drugs. The fact that these drugs are so readily available should be of concern to most people and needs to be brought to light. This study will be focusing mainly on alcohol as a gateway drug. The purpose of this study is to find if there is a connection between alcohol use and other illegal drug use.

Illicit Drug Use Among Drinkers and Nondrinkers

In 2002 and 2003, an estimated 88.2 percent of persons aged 21 or older (175.6 million) were lifetime alcohol users, whereas an estimated 11.8 percent (23.5 million) were lifetime nondrinkers. Over half of lifetime alcohol users (52.7 percent) had used one more illicit drugs at some time in their life, compared to 8.0 percent of lifetime nondrinkers. Among persons who had used an illicit drug in their lifetime, the average age at first illicit drug use was 19 years for lifetime alcohol users, versus 23 years for lifetime nondrinkers.

Lifetime alcohol users aged 21 or older had a significantly higher rate of past year illicit drug use (13.7 percent) compared with lifetime nondrinkers (2.7 percent). In addition, lifetime alcohol users had significantly higher rates of past year use across all illicit drug categories, with the exception of inhalants. Nonmedical use of pain relievers was the illicit drug used most often by lifetime nondrinkers, whereas lifetime alcohol users reported using marijuana most frequently.

Substance Abuse & Mental Health Services Administration (SAMHSA), The NSDUH Report, *January 14, 2005.*

The Study

There were 49 subjects participating in this study. Group one consisted of 15 participants. The first group was not given alcohol before they were offered fake marijuana; this was the control group. Group two consisted of 16 participants. Group two was given "shots" of alcohol so that their Blood Alcohol Content (BAC) was at the legal level for the state of Missouri (.08). Group three consisted of 18 participants. The third group was given alcohol so that their BAC was above the legal limit for driving in Missouri.

Materials include two surveys, a consent form, alcohol, and fake marijuana. The first survey asking height, weight, and gender was given along with a consent form explaining their rights before the experiment began. The second survey was given after the experiment and asked questions about participants' past and present drug use. Alcohol was given in the form of "shots". This form was used to ensure that everyone had the same amount of alcohol over the same amount of time. The marijuana used is a safe herbal supplement that looks and smells like real marijuana.

There are three groups of 15 to 18 people each being used in this study. Each group was invited over to different private residences to insure privacy. The studies were conducted over three consecutive days. Subjects were told a cover story when they arrived. They were told that they are participating in a study on alcohol to observe their behavior while intoxicated. Participants were given a consent form to read and sign. They were informed of their right to leave at any point during the experiment if they wished. They were then given a question-naire asking gender, height, and weight so that the amount of alcohol they received would be accurate for their body type. They were then given shots of alcohol according to their body weight and the group they were assigned to.

Participants were told to act as they would in a party situation. After the alcohol had time to take effect two confeder-ates began smoking "marijuana" and offered some to the rest of the group. The researchers left the room at this point. The confederates counted how many of the group choose to smoke. The confederates were instructed not to use peer pressure to get people to smoke.

Subjects were debriefed and asked to fill out a survey about their past and present drug use before leaving. Designated drivers were available for anybody receiving alcohol to insure safety.

The Results

We compared the control group to the moderate and high alcohol use groups: We predicted that the more alcohol a person has consumed the more likely they will be to want to smoke marijuana. Also, people who reported using alcohol often will also report to using marijuana. . . .

People who drank more alcohol were more likely to want to try marijuana than people who had not been drinking. 67% of the high alcohol group, 31% of the moderate alcohol group, and 6.7% of the no alcohol group tried the marijuana.

For the majority of experienced marijuana users the first drug they ever tried was alcohol. Alcohol was the first drug used by 61.3% of marijuana users. Tobacco was the first drug used by 19.4% of marijuana users. Marijuana was the first drug used by 19.4% of marijuana users.

The results of our study were statistically significant. We found that for our study the more alcohol someone drinks the more likely they will be to want to smoke marijuana. We also found that 100% of the people who reported marijuana use were also drinkers. The first drug used by the majority of people who smoke marijuana was alcohol (67%).

Anyone aged 21 or older willing to participate in this study were included. This experiment required some subjects to drink alcohol to the point of intoxication. Because of the nature of this study some potential subjects chose not to participate. We wondered if we would have gotten the same results had we used a more diverse sample. There were very few females and no minorities participating. The majority of our participants were white, male, college students.

Marijuana is called the gateway drug. It is considered the worst drug available because it supposedly causes its users to move on to harder drugs. What people don't realize is that marijuana use comes after someone is already using alcohol and tobacco.

Alcohol is easily available to all people. Unfortunately most people fail to realize that alcohol is a drug. A common misconception is that something is not a drug unless it is illegal. This mentality can potentially cause more damage than do illegal drugs. Awareness of the role of alcohol as a stepping stone needs to be brought to light through alcohol education.

| "*Less than 1 percent of adults who had never used marijuana reported heavy use of other illicit drugs.*"

Evidence Indicates That Marijuana Is a Gateway to Other Illicit Drug Use

Joseph C. Gfroerer, Li-Tzy Wu, and Michael A. Penne

In the following viewpoint, Joseph C. Gfroerer, Li-Tzy Wu, and Michael A. Penne, researching for the Substance Abuse and Mental Health Services Administration (SAMHSA), argue that there is evidence that early marijuana use is a predictor of later substance use. Specifically, the authors claim that rates of illicit substance use and abuse are higher among individuals who started using marijuana earlier than age fifteen, than for those who started using marijuana later. Joseph C. Gfroerer is a director at the Office of Applied Studies (OAS) at the Substance Abuse and Mental Health Services Administration (SAMHSA), which provides national data on alcohol, tobacco, marijuana, and other drug abuse. Li-Tzy Wu is an assistant research profes-

Joseph C. Gfroerer, Li-Tzy Wu, and Michael A. Penne, *Initiation of Marijuana Use: Trends, Patterns, and Implications*, Rockville, MD: Substance Abuse and Mental Health Services Administration (SAMHSA), Office of Applied Studies, 2002. www.oas. samhsa.gov/MJinitiation/chapter6.htm.

sor of psychiatry and behavioral science at Duke University. Michael A. Penne is a statistician and the co-author of several papers about substance abuse.

As you read, consider the following questions:

1. What is the difference in percentage of previous year cocaine use among early-onset marijuana users (use prior to age 15) and those who started using marijuana after age 20, according to the authors?
2. According to the authors, what percentage of early-onset marijuana users are heavy marijuana users, compared to those who started using marijuana after age 18?
3. What is the rate of dependence on or abuse of either alcohol or illicit drugs among early-onset marijuana users, according to the authors of the SAMHSA study?

Among adults aged 26 or older, the highest prevalence of use of heroin, cocaine, and psychotherapeutics in the lifetime was noted among those who initiated marijuana before they were 15 years old (9.2, 62.0, and 53.9 percent, respectively, for heroin, cocaine, and psychotherapeutics). There was a tendency for the prevalence of lifetime illicit drug use to decrease with older age of first marijuana use. Among lifetime marijuana users reporting their onset after age 20, an estimated 1.1 percent used heroin, 16.4 percent used cocaine, and 20.6 percent used any psychotherapeutics nonmedically in their lifetime. Among persons who had never used marijuana, less than 1 percent had ever used cocaine or heroin, but 5.1 percent had used psychotherapeutics nonmedically.

Similar patterns of past year use of these illicit drugs across the four groups of age at first marijuana use [14 or younger; 15 to 17; 18 to 20; and 21 or older] were observed. An estimated 6.9 percent of early-onset marijuana users (onset at age 14 or younger) used cocaine in the past year compared with only 0.8 percent of those initiating after age 20. An estimated

11.5 percent of early-onset marijuana users (onset at age 14 or younger) used any psychotherapeutics in the past year, while 2.9 percent of those initiating after age 20 did so.

For marijuana users aged 26 to 34 and those aged 35 to 49, rates of lifetime illicit drug use were generally higher among adolescence-onset marijuana users than among users initiating during adulthood. Because of a low prevalence of other illicit drug use among marijuana users aged 50 or older and very low proportions of past year heroin use across all three age groups (less than 1 percent), the relationship between the use of these illicit drugs and the onset age of marijuana use was less clear for them.

Heavy Illicit Drug Use

Among all lifetime marijuana users aged 26 or older, early-onset users not only had relatively higher proportions of recent (past year) heavy marijuana use than adult-onset users, but they also reported high proportions of heavy use of other illicit drugs. An estimated 5.0 percent of those initiating marijuana at age 14 or younger were recent heavy marijuana users compared with less than 1 percent of those with an onset age of 18 years or older. Likewise, 6.3 percent of those initiating marijuana at age 14 or younger were recent heavy users of other illicit drugs in comparison with about 1 percent of those with an onset age of 18 years or older. A similar pattern also was observed among two age groups of marijuana users (i.e., adults aged 26 to 34 and those aged 35 to 49). There was an insufficient number of heavy illicit drug users among the older age group (i.e., aged 50 or older) to allow for such a comparison. Less than 1 percent of adults who had never used marijuana reported heavy use of other illicit drugs. . . .

Substance Dependence and/or Abuse

Overall and among those aged 26 to 49, prevalence rates of dependence on or abuse of an illicit drug and prevalence rates of dependence on or abuse of either alcohol or an illicit drug

Marijuana Is a Gateway to Harder Drugs

A direct cause-and-effect relationship between marijuana use and subsequent use of other drugs is hard to prove. Studies show, however, that of the people who have ever used marijuana, those who started early are more likely to have other problems later on. For example, adults who were early marijuana users were found to be:

- 8 times more likely to have used cocaine;

- 15 times more likely to have used heroin;

- 5 times more likely to develop a need for treatment of abuse or dependence on *any* drug.

The *Journal of the American Medical Association* reported a study of more than 300 sets of same-sex twins. The study found that marijuana-using twins were four times more likely than their siblings to use cocaine and crack cocaine, and five times more likely to use hallucinogens such as LSD.

Office of National Drug Control Policy (ONDCP),
"What Americans Need to Know About Marijuana," October 2003.

were highest among those who started to use marijuana at age 14 or younger. An estimated 6.2 percent of those initiating marijuana before age 15 abused or were dependent on an illicit drug in the past year compared with 1.3 percent of those initiating marijuana at age 21 or older. Similarly, 18.0 percent of early-onset (onset before age 15) marijuana users were classified with dependence on or abuse of either alcohol or an illicit drug in comparison with 7.6 percent of those who first used marijuana after age 20.

Even when the prevalence was restricted to dependence and was specific to alcohol, an illicit drug, marijuana, or an illicit drug other than marijuana, prevalence rates of dependence for each outcome were consistently found to be highest among marijuana users who started their first use at age 14 or younger.

Among adults who had never used marijuana, the prevalence of past year alcohol and/or illicit drug abuse or dependence was very low. Only about 0.2 percent of them were classified with dependence on or abuse of an illicit drug and 0.9 percent were dependent on alcohol. In addition, there was a tendency among those who had never used marijuana for the prevalence of illicit drug abuse or dependence to be higher among young adults aged 26 to 34 years (0.4 percent), but for the prevalence of alcohol dependence to be slightly higher among persons aged 35 to 49 (1.4 percent).

| *"The lie that marijuana somehow turns people into junkies is dead."*

Marijuana Is Not a Gateway Drug

Bruce Mirken

In the following viewpoint, Bruce Mirken argues that the gateway theory, which states that use of tobacco, alcohol, and marijuana leads to the use of "hard" drugs, has been refuted. Mirken points to two recent studies, neither of which find factual evidence of a gateway theory. The author concludes that we can no longer use the alleged gateway effect of marijuana as justification for keeping it illegal. Bruce Mirken is communications director for the Marijuana Policy Project, the largest marijuana policy reform organization in the United States.

As you read, consider the following questions:

1. What were the findings regarding tobacco, alcohol, and marijuana use among 224 boys involved in a study at the University of Pittsburgh?

2. What did the study of Australian twins conclude about the cause of marijuana use and other drug use?

Bruce Mirken, "Seriously, Man, Pot Won't Make You a Junkie," *Chicago Sun-Times*, December 24, 2006. Copyright © 2006 *Chicago Sun-Times*. Reproduced by permission of the author.

3. What did the researchers conclude is the actual cause of any perceived gateway effect of marijuana?

Two recent studies should be the final nails in the coffin of the lie that has propelled some of this nation's most misguided policies: the claim that smoking marijuana somehow causes people to use hard drugs, often called the "gateway theory."

Such claims have been a staple of the White House Office of National Drug Control Policy under present [2006] drug czar John Walters. Typical is a 2004 New Mexico speech in which, according to the *Albuquerque Journal*, "Walters emphasized that marijuana is a 'gateway drug' that can lead to other chemical dependencies." The gateway theory presents drug use as a tidy progression in which users move from legal drugs like alcohol and tobacco to marijuana, and from there to hard drugs like cocaine, heroin and methamphetamine. Thus, zealots like Waiters warn, marijuana is bad because it leads to things that are even worse.

It's a neat theory, easy to sell. The problem is, scientists keep poking holes in it—the two new studies being [released] are just the most recent examples.

Research Denies a Gateway Effect

In one National Institute on Drug Abuse-funded study, researchers from the University of Pittsburgh tracked the drug use patterns of 224 boys, starting at age 10 to 12 and ending at age 22. Right from the beginning these kids confounded expectations. Some followed the traditional gateway paradigm, starting with tobacco or alcohol and moving on to marijuana, but some reversed the pattern, starting with marijuana first. And some never progressed from one substance to another at all.

When they looked at the detailed data on these kids, the researchers found that the gateway theory simply didn't hold;

Study Raises Questions about Drug-Use Sequence

The gateway hypothesis holds that abusable drugs occupy distinct ranks in a hierarchy as well as definite positions in a temporal sequence. Accordingly, substance use is theorized to progress through a sequence of stages, beginning with legal, socially acceptable compounds that are low in the hierarchy, followed by use of illegal "soft" and later "hard" drugs ranked higher in the hierarchy. One of the main findings of this study is that there is a high rate of nonconformance with this temporal order. In a neighborhood where there is high drug availability, youths who have low parental supervision are likely to regularly consume marijuana before alcohol and/or tobacco. Consumption of marijuana prior to use of licit drugs thus appears to be related contextual factors rather than to any unique characteristics of the individual. Moreover, this reverse pattern is not rare; it was observed in over 20% of our sample.

Ralph E. Tarter, et al, "Predictors of Marijuana Use in Adolescents Before and After Licit Drug Use: Examination of the Gateway Hypothesis," The American Journal of Psychiatry, *December 2006.*

environmental factors such as neighborhood characteristics played a much larger role than which drug the boys happened to use first. "Abusable drugs," they wrote, "occupy neither a specific place in a hierarchy nor a discrete position in a temporal sequence."

Lead researcher Dr. Ralph E. Tarter told the *Pittsburgh Post-Gazette*, "It runs counter to about six decades of current drug policy in the country, where we believe that if we can't stop kids from using marijuana, then they're going to go on and become addicts to hard drugs."

Researchers in Brisbane, Australia, and St. Louis reached much the same conclusion in a larger and more complex study published last month [November 2006] The research involved more than 4,000 Australian twins whose use of marijuana and other drugs was followed in detail from adolescence into adulthood.

Then—and here's the fascinating part—they matched the real-world data from the twins to mathematical models based on 13 different explanations of how use of marijuana and other illicit drugs might be related. These models ranged from pure chance—assuming that any overlap between use of marijuana and other drugs is random—to models in which underlying genetic or environmental factors lead to both marijuana and other drug use or model in which marijuana use causes use of other drugs or vice versa.

When they crunched the numbers, only one conclusion made sense: "Cannabis and other illicit drug use and misuse co-occur in the population due to common risk factors (correlated vulnerabilities) or a liability that is in part shared." Translated to plain English: the data don't show that marijuana causes use of other drugs, but instead indicate that the same factors that make people likely to try marijuana also make them likely to try other substances.

Research Supports Legalizing Marijuana

In the final blow to claims that marijuana must remain illegal to keep us from becoming a nation of hard-drug addicts, the researchers added that any gateway effect that does exist is "more likely to be social than pharmacological," occurring because marijuana "introduces users to a provider (peer or black marketeer) who eventually becomes the source for other illicit drugs." In other words, the gateway isn't marijuana; it's laws that put marijuana into the same criminal underground with speed and heroin.

The lie that marijuana somehow turns people into junkies is dead. Officials who insist on repeating it as a way of squelching discussion about common-sense reforms should be laughed off the stage.

Periodical Bibliography

The following articles have been selected to supplement the diverse views presented in this chapter.

Doug Brunk — "Stimulants for ADHD: No Link to Later Drug Abuse," *Family Practice News*, October 1, 2005.

David M. Fergusson, Joseph M. Boden, and L. John Horwood — "Cannabis Use and Other Illicit Drug Use: Testing the Cannabis Gateway Hypothesis," *Addiction*, April 2006.

Kimberly L. Henry, Michael D. Slater, and Eugene R. Oetting — "Alcohol Use in Early Adolescence: The Effect of Changes in Risk Taking, Perceived Harm and Friends' Alcohol Use," *Journal of Studies on Alcohol*, March 2005.

Denise B. Kandel — "Does Marijuana Use Cause the Use of Other Drugs?" The *Journal of the American Medical Association*, January 22, 2003.

Lesley W. Reid, Kirk W. Elifson, and Claire E. Sterk — "Ecstasy and Gateway Drugs: Initiating the Use of Ecstasy and Other Drugs," *Annals of Epidemiology*, 2007.

Anita Srikameswaran — "Researchers Say Smoking Pot Not Always Path to Hard Drugs Drug Use," *Pittsburgh Post-Gazette*, December 05, 2006.

Ralph E. Tarter et al. — "Predictors of Marijuana Use in Adolescents Before and After Licit Drug Use: Examination of the Gateway Hypothesis," *American Journal of Psychiatry*, December 2006.

Patrick Zickler — "Twins Study Links Early Marijuana Use to Increased Risk of Abuse or Dependence," *NIDA Notes*, November 2003.

CHAPTER 4

What Should Society Do About Gateway Drugs?

Chapter Preface

Determining whether certain drugs are harmful—whether through immediate effects to the user and others, or by a gateway effect leading to the use of other drugs that are harmful—is one of the key steps in deciding what sort of policies society ought to take toward drug use. Legality is one issue, of course. But once a drug is legal, there are also considerations of how to regulate and monitor use.

Tobacco and alcohol are examples of two drugs that, though legal, are regulated in terms of age of use, content of products, and place of consumption. In order to justify the legality of these substances, one need not necessarily argue that they are harmless—many of the tobacco and alcohol regulations are in place to mitigate dangers to users and others. Nonetheless, many substances are considered too harmful and without redeeming social value to be tolerated. Marijuana, heroin, cocaine, crack, LSD, and methamphetamine are some examples of substances in this class. Alcohol, for a brief time, was a forbidden substance in the United States.

In 1919, ratification was completed for the Eighteenth Amendment of the United States Constitution, with the era known as Prohibition beginning one year later on January 16, 1920. The Eighteenth Amendment prohibited the "manufacture, sale, or transportation of intoxicating liquors within, the importation thereof into, or the exportation thereof from the United States." Alcohol remained illegal until the end of 1933, when the Twenty-First Amendment repealed the Eighteenth Amendment. Prohibition ended, at least in part, because of the high public demand for alcohol, in spite of its legal status, and the organized crime that emerged as a result of this demand. In this sense, the prohibition policy was a failure because it did not stop the consumption of alcohol and, many would say, resulted in even greater problems.

The conclusions drawn from the failure of Prohibition are varied. Ethan Nadelmann believes that Prohibition showed that the harms of outlawing a substance can sometimes be worse than the harms of allowing the substance: "The Americans who voted in 1933 to repeal Prohibition differed greatly in their reasons for overturning the system. They almost all agreed, however, that the evils of alcohol consumption had been surpassed by those trying to suppress it." He goes on to use this as an analogical argument for the conclusion that marijuana laws do more harm than allowing marijuana use. On the other hand, Gene Amondson, member of the Prohibition Party and 2004 presidential candidate, argues that the Prohibition years were America's best years and that we ought to outlaw alcohol again.

In the following chapter, the authors examine different policies toward tobacco, alcohol, and marijuana. The policies considered include measures as extreme as arguing for an outlaw of a particular substance, like alcohol during Prohibition, to consideration of partial bans and other regulations.

> "Put marijuana where it belongs, in li-
> censed and regulated outlets as we do
> with alcohol."

Marijuana Is Not Any More Dangerous than Alcohol and Should Be Legalized

Ray Warren

In the following viewpoint, Ray Warren argues that current pro-hibition of marijuana is fueled by fear. Warren suggests that marijuana be regulated in the same way as alcohol and suggests that current policies toward marijuana are not in the best inter-est of the public. He asserts that an Institute of Medicine study refuted the theory that the biochemical effects of marijuana lead to hard-drug use. Ray Warren is director of state policies for the Marijuana Policy Project in Washington, D.C. He is a former member of the North Carolina house of representatives and a former judge.

As you read, consider the following questions:

1. How many people under the age of fifty-five does the author suggest know somebody who uses or has used marijuana?

Ray Warren, "So Little to Fear in Legal Marijuana," *News & Observer*, July 20, 2007. www.mpp.org. Reproduced by permission.

2. What legal substance does the author claim is more toxic and dangerous to society than marijuana?

3. According to the author, what does it mean that most people do not "turn in" people they know who are breaking the law by using marijuana?

Justice John Paul Stevens recently asked in a U.S. Supreme Court opinion "whether the fear of disapproval by those in the majority is silencing opponents of the war on drugs." The answer is a resounding "yes," though it's not at all clear that a majority actually agrees with current policies regarding marijuana regulation. Fear of being called "soft on drugs" is stifling rational debate about the relative merits of prohibition vs. regulation of a substance most regard as relatively innocuous.

Marijuana Policy Fueled by Fear

Virtually everyone under the age 55 knows somebody who uses or has used marijuana. Many need only look in a mirror. Yet federal and state governments continue to treat marijuana possession as a serious crime. This is a wildly disproportionate response, fueled by fear, to an activity that is widespread among all classes of society.

As part of an organization seeking to reform prohibition-oriented marijuana laws, I witness this phenomenon daily. Legislators acknowledge privately that current policies are not working, but fret that voters will not accept reform. Citizens wink and nod at marijuana use by loved ones while supporting laws that could ruin their loved ones' lives. Everybody is afraid to question current policies.

Instead of acting like Chicken Little, perhaps we should ask ourselves exactly what would happen if marijuana was regulated like alcohol. That might make for calm and rational public policy decisions.

Far too many people have tried marijuana, or know somebody who has used it, for the public to really believe in the

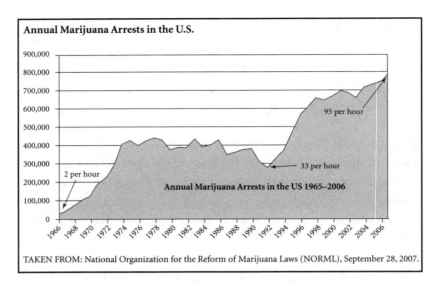

Annual Marijuana Arrests in the U.S.

95 per hour

2 per hour

Annual Marijuana Arrests in the US 1965–2006

33 per hour

TAKEN FROM: National Organization for the Reform of Marijuana Laws (NORML), September 28, 2007.

"Reefer Madness" stories circulated by government fear-mongers. As with alcohol, some people would abuse marijuana. But, also as with alcohol, most would adjust their consumption in a responsible manner.

Treat Marijuana like Alcohol

Every day the papers are full of stories of misery wrought by overindulgence in alcohol—a substance more toxic, and far more likely to induce violence or aggression, than marijuana. Yet prohibition is not considered a serious response to alcohol abuse. And in the real world, most people don't drink themselves into oblivion daily, despite the relative ease and low expense involved in doing so.

But if we regulated marijuana like alcohol, what message would that send to our children? Good question. What message do we send when we enact laws that punish a few unlucky individuals for doing what much of the population does without punishment?

We cannot engender respect for the law by criminalizing private behavior while quietly tolerating the flouting of the law. Experience with alcohol prohibition taught us that.

But isn't marijuana a "gateway" to other drugs? Not through its biochemical effects, as the Institute of Medicine noted in its White House-funded study. The "gateway" is the suppliers—drug dealers who peddle other drugs as well. Put an attractive product in the same market basket as hard drugs and shoppers may sample the other products. Put marijuana where it belongs, in licensed and regulated outlets as we do with alcohol, and consumers won't see the drug dealers' other wares.

Bourbon is sold by legal venues where identification is checked, and proprietors have reason to follow rules in order to preserve their liquor licenses. The fact that marijuana is illegal creates a completely unregulated market where anything goes.

Lives Ruined by Marijuana Policies

I've been licensed to practice law in North Carolina for nearly 25 years. I had the privilege of serving as a Superior Court judge for seven and one half of those years. I wouldn't know where to buy marijuana if I had to. And my own experience with it is limited to the casual exposure nearly every adult under 55 has had. But I've seen many lives ruined by misguided policies that treat the consumption of marijuana as a major threat to society.

If we really believe that our friends, family and neighbors are ruining their own lives and threatening the public safety, we should turn them in immediately. The fact that most of us do not do that is testament to the fact we really don't perceive marijuana as a threat to the public order.

Properly regulating and taxing marijuana for adult use would save millions of dollars in law enforcement, court costs and correction department spending. It would also bring in millions in tax revenues for education, roads and other critical needs, and shut a "gateway" to hard drugs.

Ignoring that opportunity based on hysterical fears about a substance few view as a threat to public order is true "reefer madness."

"Ending all prohibition on cannabis and all other drugs is not saying 'yes' to drugs."

Marijuana Has Dangers but Should Be Legalized

Rosie Boycott

In the following viewpoint, Rosie Boycott argues that her position in favor of the legalization of cannabis, or marijuana, has not changed, even though her belief about the harmfulness of marijuana has changed. She asserts that skunk, a high-potency type of marijuana widely available in Great Britain today, is far more dangerous than the marijuana smoked in the past. Rather than seeing this development as a reason to change her mind about decriminalization, she sees it as an additional argument to support legalization and improve regulation of the drug. Rosie Boycott, is a journalist and the former editor of The Independent. *Since the late 1990s, she has been involved in the movement to decriminalize cannabis, or marijuana, in Great Britain.*

As you read, consider the following questions:

1. According to the author, what were the main points behind the campaign to decriminalize cannabis in 1997?

2. What are some of the dangers of the stronger marijuana available now, according to the author?

3. Why does the author claim that full legalization of marijuana is more important now than ever?

I smoked my first joint in the summer of 1968. I was 17 and it was the summer of love: hot, sexy, the Rolling Stones performing for free in Hyde Park and the dope was plentiful and benign. It would come in from Lebanon, Morocco or Afghanistan and I'd buy it in small lumps which looked and crumbled just like Oxo cubes.

Sitting on the grass in Hyde Park, armed with a packet of cigarette papers and the contents of a Benson & Hedges, I rolled my first joint. The dope made me happy. It seemed such a much better way to get high than my parents' nightly tipple of sherry or dry martinis.

The Campaign to Decriminalize Marijuana

Everyone I knew in those days smoked pot and most people I know now have smoked at least once in their lives: some of them now run corporations and political parties, and there is no evidence that smoking pot ever hurt them. When I began a campaign to decriminalise cannabis at *The Independent on Sunday* in 1997 we were greeted with derision by the powers that be. Alastair Campbell memorably described us as a "bunch of old hippies still living in the Sixties".

But our campaign quickly attracted the attention of police officers, prison wardens and teachers who were by no means just a bunch of old hippies. Our points were simple: cannabis does less harm than alcohol; it does not lead people to violence, and no one smokes themselves to death (as they might drink themselves to death). Cannabis, not in itself an addictive drug, does not lead people to hard drugs but the criminalisation of it means that the person who sells you pot has a vested interest in leading you towards much more harmful

The War on Marijuana

Over the past two decades billions of dollars have been spent fighting the war on marijuana, millions of Americans have been arrested and tens of thousands have been imprisoned. Has it been worth it? According to the government's National Household Survey on Drug Abuse, in 1982 about 54 percent of Americans between the ages of 18 and 25 had smoked marijuana. In 2002 the proportion was . . . about 54 percent.

Eric Schlosser, "Make Peace with Pot,"
New York Times, April 26, 2004.

and potentially addictive substances. Locking up young kids because they smoked dope meant we were making criminals of people who were, I believe, no more criminal than my sherry-tippling mother.

Our campaigning worked. In time the law was changed and cannabis was reclassified, making possession barely against the law. I am glad about this because I do not believe that we can ever contain the drug trade by making outlaws of the users and by allowing criminal gangs to control the supply.

Marijuana Is Not Harmless Today

But in one respect I have changed my mind. In 1997, I was confident that cannabis was an almost harmless drug. No drug, even caffeine, can be said to be entirely without its dangers. But I was talking about the pot that comes from the sun-filled fields of the Lebanon, Morocco and Afghanistan. Today's 30-times stronger variety—known as skunk—has been definitively linked with paranoid schizophrenia and psychosis, mostly among teenage boys who smoke heavily. It is now the most common form of the drug available on our streets because it can be grown so easily at home. . . .

Last summer I visited a hydroponic supply store in north London located behind a piano shop. The piano area was musty and dimly lit, but once through a small door in the back, I was in something that was part garden centre, part pharmacy and part chemical repository.

Strange bits of furniture which outwardly resembled portable wardrobes opened up to reveal a complex system of lights and plastic tubes which carry fertilisers to the plants. By alternating light levels and a judicious use of chemicals, you can go from seed to plant in just eight weeks. The outlay is negligible. A single plant produces about an ounce of skunk, which costs between £100 and £120 on the street.

The dope I used to smoke that we campaigned to have legalised is now a rarity. Why bother with all the problems of importation if you can grow it in your bedroom as easily as I grew mustard and cress on blotting paper when I was a kid at school?

Psychologist Julie Lynn-Evans, who works with teenagers who have developed paranoia and schizophrenia from smoking dope, says that she would rather her children became addicted to heroin than skunk. At least you can completely recover from a heroin problem, whereas skunk can leave lasting damage. Teenage boys, whose brains mature later than those of girls, are particularly vulnerable.

Hearing voices is a familiar symptom. While researching a TV programme on the subject last year, I met a 20-year-old patient of Julie's and I asked him what the voices said. "Just real absolute junk . . . they don't want me to do that to them and I don't want them doing it to me but . . ." He talked about them as though they were real. To him they were holding conversations in his head which could go on for weeks, telling him he was no good, reinforcing messages of paranoia and low self-esteem.

Julie says that it is the most serious stuff on our streets to-day: "Once it has hit the frontal lobes of the developing adolescent, you just don't know whether they'll recover or not."

The Dangers Support Legalization

But how are people to know just what they are smoking? Teenagers are always going to smoke cannabis, just as they will always indulge in under-age drinking. But on today's chaotic streets, where cannabis doesn't come with a product-information label, it's like entering an off-licence and asking for a pint of alcohol without knowing whether you're buying beer or tequila.

The real dangers of skunk do not change my mind about legalisation. Indeed, I now think full legalisation to be more important, so that there can be sensible education about the possible dangers. We can never, ever hope to give out clear, straightforward educational messages about drugs while they remain illegal. We have no chance of ever controlling how drugs are sold and who they are sold to. Illegality drives the drug trade underground, exposing users to drugs—not just cannabis—of fluctuating strength and dubious origin, randomly dangerous in their inconsistencies.

Ending all prohibition on cannabis and all other drugs is not saying "yes" to drugs. Today's skunk is far cheaper and far more potent than what I smoked as a 20-year-old. And we are all paying an increasingly high price.

Unlike the old-fashioned cannabis of my youth, skunk makes people aggressive: they steal, break into cars and snatch phones. It makes everyone the victim but the true losers are our sons and daughters who literally, where skunk is concerned, risk losing their minds and themselves.

| *"It is time to explode the myth of cannabis as a 'soft' drug."*

Marijuana Is Dangerous and Should Not Be Legalized

Antonio Maria Costa

In the following viewpoint, Antonio Maria Costa argues that marijuana is portrayed falsely as a harmless substance that should be legalized. In contrast, Costa claims that marijuana's potential harms justify strict control of the substance. Costa claims that stricter policies and enforcement of laws can eliminate many of the negative effects countries suffer as a result of marijuana. Antonio Maria Costa is executive director of the United Nations Office on Drugs and Crime (UNODC).

As you read, consider the following questions:

1. According to the author, how has the concentration of THC in marijuana changed over the last several decades?

2. What is one way that people besides the users of marijuana can be harmed by marijuana consumption, according to the author?

3. In what ways does the author think that Sweden is an excellent example of a country with good drug policies?

Seldom does a leading newspaper take a high-profile stand in favour of drug liberalisation. It is less common still for such a campaign to be publicly retracted. *The Independent on Sunday* deserves great credit for having the courage to change its mind on cannabis on the basis of mounting evidence of just how dangerous the world's most popular illicit drug has become.

Marijuana Is Not Harmless

It cannot have been an easy decision. Many readers undoubtedly subscribe to the vague, laissez-faire tolerance of cannabis increasingly prevalent among educated people in Western countries. That growing consensus needs to be challenged. Supporters of legalisation would have us believe that cannabis is a gentle, harmless substance that gives users little more than a sense of mellow euphoria and hurts no one else. It's not an unattractive image. Sellers of "skunk" know better. Trawl through websites offering cannabis seeds for sale and you will find brand names such as Armageddon, AK-47 and White Widow. "This will put you in pieces, then reduce you to rubble—maybe quicksand if you go too far," one Glasgow-based seller boasts. This is much closer to the truth.

The cannabis now in circulation is many times more powerful than the weed that today's ageing baby-boomers smoked in college. In the flower-power era, the concentration of THC, as the main psychoactive substance in cannabis is known, was typically 2 or 3 per cent. Present-day cannabis can contain 10 times as much.

Today's skunk is a product of several developments in cannabis cultivation: the "sinsemilla technique" (the cultivation of only unfertilised female plants); the use of indoor growing technologies; and the use of plant strains bred for higher yield and potency.

Marijuana Dangers

Cannabis does not produce physical dependency, as does heroin, but some people who use it regularly can become psychologically dependent. Cannabis smoke is carcinogenic, and so can contribute to lung cancer, just like tobacco smoke. And regular smoking can exacerbate existing respiratory problems, such as asthma, bronchitis and wheezing.

A few studies have suggested that regular users may also have impaired immune systems, and there is little doubt that driving while stoned is dangerous—one study found that smoking cannabis doubles the risk of fatal car crashes. According to a study in *The Lancet*, large doses of THC produce confusion, amnesia, delusions, hallucinations, anxiety and agitation.

Steve Connor, The Independent, *June 28, 2006.*

Evidence of the damage to mental health caused by cannabis use—from loss of concentration to paranoia, aggressiveness and outright psychosis—is mounting and cannot be ignored. Emergency-room admissions involving cannabis are rising, as is demand for rehabilitation treatment.

The Reasons for Marijuana Control

Amid all the libertarian talk about the right of individuals to engage in dangerous practices provided no one else gets hurt, certain key facts are easily forgotten. First, cannabis is a dangerous drug—not just to the individuals who use it. People who drive under the influence of cannabis put others at risk. Would even the most ardent supporter of legalisation want to fly in an aircraft whose pilot used cannabis?

Second, drug control works. More than a century of universally accepted restrictions on heroin and cocaine have prevented a pandemic. Global levels of drug addiction—think of the opium dens of the 19th century—have dropped dramatically in the past 100 years. In the past 10 years or so, they have remained stable. The drug problem is being contained and our societies are safer and healthier as a result.

The exception is cannabis, the weakest link in the chain. It is a weed that grows under the most varied conditions in many countries, which makes supply control difficult. But we can tackle demand, especially among the young. That need not mean sending them to jail. Young people caught in possession of cannabis could be treated in much the same way as those arrested for drunk driving—fined, required to attend classes on the dangers of drug use and threatened with loss of their driving licence for repeat offences.

Drug Problems Reflect Drug Policies

I am increasingly convinced countries get the drug problem they deserve. Those that invest political capital—backed by adequate resources—in prevention, treatment and rehabilitation are rewarded with significantly lower rates of drug abuse.

Sweden is an excellent example. Drug use is just a third of the European average while spending on drug control is three times the EU average. For three decades, Sweden has had consistent and coherent drug-control policies, regardless of which party is in power. There is a strong emphasis on prevention, drug laws have been progressively tightened, and extensive treatment and rehabilitation opportunities are available to users. The police take drug crime seriously.

Governments and societies must keep their nerve and avoid being swayed by misguided notions of tolerance. They must not lose sight of the fact that illicit drugs are dangerous—that is why the world agreed to restrict them.

The global cannabis market is changing. Traditional suppliers to the UK such as Morocco—the world's largest producer of cannabis resin—are slashing cultivation. That is more than offset by an increase in home-grown cannabis, now the main source of supply for most major markets. In Britain, demand will increasingly be met by well-organised indoor production with links to criminal networks. This represents a growing challenge for police.

Drug prevention and treatment will need to change in response to the effects of more powerful cannabis varieties on cognitive capacity, memory and emotional development, as well as schizophrenia among vulnerable individuals exposed to the drug. Public attitudes also need to change. The IoS [*Independent on Sunday*] has provided a valuable lead. It is time to explode the myth of cannabis as a "soft" drug.

| "Smoking tobacco should be outlawed,
  clear and simple."

Tobacco Use Should
Be Outlawed

John W. Whitehead

In the following viewpoint, John W. Whitehead argues that tobacco smoking should be made illegal. Whitehead asserts that tobacco is the most dangerous drug in the United States. It is the corrupt influence of the tobacco industry's political contributions and lobbying that explain why it is not illegal, he claims. John W. Whitehead, president of the Rutherford Institute, is an attorney and author who has written, debated, and practiced widely in the area of constitutional law and human rights.

As you read, consider the following questions:

1. According to the report Whitehead cites, male smokers and female smokers cut their live short by how many years, respectively?

2. How much money did the tobacco industry spend on lobbying for each day Congress was in session in 2003, according to the author?

John W. Whitehead, "Death in a Cigarette: Tobacco Smoking Should Be Outlawed," The Rutherford Institute, June 7, 2004. www.rutherford.org. Reproduced by permission.

3. According to Whitehead, when do most smokers start smoking tobacco?

Every day, the U.S. government spends millions of dollars in its efforts to prevent illegal drugs from entering this country. The Bush Administration even has a spirited campaign against marijuana, going so far as to fight medicinal marijuana use and any product that may have a trace of hemp in it. However, while the most frightful and dangerous drug on the planet rages in the bodies of millions of Americans, including a large segment of our young people, our government is doing virtually nothing to stop it.

Tobacco Is a Lethal Drug

Indeed, the U.S. Surgeon General has recently released a comprehensive report on smoking and health. It reveals for the first time that smoking causes diseases in nearly every organ of the human body. Published 40 years after the Surgeon General's first report on smoking—which concluded that smoking was a definite cause of three serious diseases (lung and larynx cancer and chronic bronchitis)—this newest report finds that cigarette smoking is conclusively linked to diseases such as leukemia, cataracts, pneumonia and cancers of the cervix, kidney, pancreas and stomach.

According to this new report, smoking kills an estimated 440,000 Americans each year. On average, men who smoke cut their lives short by 13.2 years, and female smokers lose 14.5 years. The economic toll exceeds $157 billion each year in the United States—$75 billion in direct medical costs and $82 billion in lost productivity.

Statistics indicate that more than 12 million Americans have died from smoking since the 1964 report of the Surgeon General. Moreover, another 25 million Americans alive today will most likely die of smoking-related illnesses. And it doesn't matter what type of cigarette is smoked. In fact, another ma-

Health Hazards of Tobacco

Since 1964, 28 Surgeon General's reports on smoking and health have concluded that tobacco use is the single most avoidable cause of disease, disability, and death in the United States. In 1988, the Surgeon General concluded that cigarettes and other forms of tobacco, such as cigars, pipe tobacco, and chewing tobacco, are addictive and that nicotine is the drug in tobacco that causes addiction. Nicotine provides an almost immediate "kick" because it causes a discharge of epinephrine from the adrenal cortex. This stimulates the central nervous system and endocrine glands, which causes a sudden release of glucose. Stimulation is then followed by depression and fatigue, leading the user to seek more nicotine.

Nicotine is absorbed readily from tobacco smoke in the lungs, and it does not matter whether the tobacco smoke is from cigarettes, cigars, or pipes. Nicotine also is absorbed readily when tobacco is chewed. With regular use of tobacco, levels of nicotine accumulate in the body during the day and persist overnight. Thus, daily smokers or chewers are exposed to the effects of nicotine for 24 hours each day.

National Institute on Drugs Abuse (NIDA),
"Cigarettes and Other Tobacco Products," July 2006.

jor conclusion from the latest report, consistent with recent findings of other scientific studies, is that smoking so-called low-tar or low-nicotine cigarettes does not offer any health benefits over smoking regular or "full-flavor" cigarettes. "There is no safe cigarette, whether it is called 'light,' 'ultra-light' or any other name," the Surgeon General has said. "The science is clear: the only way to avoid the health hazards of smoking is to quit completely or to never start smoking."

Why Tobacco Is Legal

The obvious question is: If tobacco is the most lethal and dangerous drug in the United States, why is it not greatly curtailed or even made illegal? To find the answer, one need look no further than political contributions.

The tobacco industry has made more than $1.8 million in political contributions to federal candidates, political parties and political committees so far in 2003–2004. And, according to a quarterly report issued by the Campaign for Tobacco-Free Kids Action Fund and Common Cause, since 1997, the tobacco industry has contributed more than $27.7 million to various political action committees. And since 1999, tobacco companies have also spent more than $101 million on lobbying the U.S. Congress. Indeed, the tobacco industry spent more than $21.2 million to lobby Congress in 2003. That amounts to approximately $127,000 spent on lobbying for every day that Congress was in session.

The report from the Campaign for Tobacco-Free Kids Action Fund demonstrates how the tobacco industry's contributions are used to thwart public health policy. The report details contributions to the sponsors and co-sponsors of legislation that would provide for regulation of tobacco products by the Food and Drug Administration. In fact, the 17 House members who sponsored legislation opposed by the public health industry received, on average, more than 20 times as much money from the tobacco industry than the 127 sponsors of public health conscious legislation.

One is tempted to argue that the lobbying process as used by the tobacco companies is democracy in action. However, at base it is the rawest form of political corruption when big money buys the loyalty of members of Congress and forces a nefarious silence from our president and other political leaders. As William V. Corr, executive director of the Campaign for Tobacco-Free Kids Action Fund said when releasing his study, "Today's report tells us why there has been so little action on tobacco in Congress, despite the fact that more than 2,000 kids become addicted smokers every day and more than 400,000 Americans die every year from tobacco use."

Sadly, nearly 90 percent of smokers begin at or before age 18. Those who peddle the death that is tobacco target young smokers in the hopes of hooking human beings on tobacco for the rest of their lives. And as we're finding, the only outcome is sickness and death.

What Should Be Done About Tobacco

So, what should be done? Smoking tobacco should be outlawed, clear and simple. Why would we settle for anything less?

| *"A nonsmoking majority cannot arbitrarily stamp out the rights of a smoking minority."*

The Government Imposes Too Many Restrictions on the Rights of Smokers

Robert A. Levy

In the following viewpoint, Robert A. Levy argues that smoking bans impinge on the rights of smokers. Discussing a proposed smoking ban on the beaches of California, Levy shows why three arguments in favor of the ban fail: he denies that the prevention of littering, the prevention of the health hazard of secondhand smoke, or the will of the majority succeed as justifications for the beach smoking ban. Robert A. Levy is senior fellow in constitutional studies at the Cato Institute in Washington, D.C.

As you read, consider the following questions:

1. In what way does the author think a beach smoking ban is both over-inclusive and under-inclusive?

2. What evidence does Levy cite in support of his claim that secondhand smoke is not a health hazard?

3. What does the author claim is required for a regulation, such as a smoking ban, to be legitimate?

Here we go again. First it was the health police in Santa Monica, Los Angeles and Malibu. Then the buttheads in Los Angeles County. Now it's the legislature, about to consider a bill to shield every sun worshipper statewide from the tribulations of beach smoking, and defend every grain of sand along the 1,100-mile coastline against cigarette litter.

One argument for the beach ban goes like this: Cigarette butts are a major source of litter. On cleanup days, volunteers say they pick up an average of more than 300,000 butts along the beach. If so, that's a powerful argument—but against littering, not against smoking. A ban on smoking is both over-inclusive and under-inclusive. It's over-inclusive because responsible smokers who properly discard their cigarette butts do not contribute to litter. It's under-inclusive because irresponsible non-smokers who improperly discard food wrappers and soda cans are major contributors to litter. By all means, let's keep the beaches clean. Anyone who flips a cigarette butt onto the sand may deserve to be fined. But let's reserve our ire, and our legal remedies, for those who actually do something wrong.

The Secondhand Smoke Argument

The second argument against beach smoking is that secondhand smoke, even a wisp on breezy days, is a health hazard. The short answer is that no evidence exists to support that bald assertion. Indeed, a substantial body of evidence cuts the other way. In 1996, the American Heart Association journal, *Circulation*, reported no increase in coronary heart disease associated with secondhand smoke "at work or in other settings." Two years later, the World Health Organization reported "no association between childhood exposure to environmental tobacco smoke [ETS] and lung cancer." A 1999 editorial in *The New England Journal of Medicine* concluded,

State-Sponsored Behavior Modification

I often take the train from Washington, D.C., to New York and back. A few years ago they put the smoking car on the end of the train so nonsmokers wouldn't have to go through it to get to other parts of the train. And then the day came when they said, "We're taking that car off the train altogether." And I thought, "Now we've crossed a small but important line." It's the difference between protecting nonsmokers and state-sponsored behavior modification for smokers.

And I thought there was insufficient alarm at the ease with which that was done. Because state behavior modification, no matter what its object, should be viewed skeptically at the very least. There's serious danger in the imposition of uniformity—the suggestion that one size must fit all.

Christopher Hitchens, Cato Policy Report, *March/April 2006.*

"We still do not know, with accuracy, how much or even whether [ETS] increases the risk of coronary heart disease."

Then there's the granddaddy of all secondhand smoke studies: the landmark 1993 report by the Environmental Protection Agency declaring that ETS is a dangerous carcinogen that causes 3,000 deaths annually. Five years later, a federal judge lambasted EPA for "cherry picking" the data, excluding studies that "demonstrated no association between ETS and cancer," and withholding "significant portions of its findings and reasoning in striving to confirm its *a priori* hypothesis."

More recently, in the May 2003 *British Medical Journal,* researchers found that passive smoke had no significant connection with heart-disease or lung-cancer death at any level of exposure at any time. Those results, stated the American

Council on Science and Health, are "consistent" with studies by the Centers for Disease Control and Prevention.

The Rights of the Minority

So what?, you might argue. Maybe secondhand smoke doesn't kill people, but how about the harm to people with pre-existing asthma, respiratory infections, or eye allergies? After all, public beaches belong collectively to the citizens of a community. Why shouldn't those citizens decide, through their elected representatives, what conduct is permissible and what is not? Why should a minority of smokers be able to dictate public policy to a majority of non-smokers?

Ordinarily, in a democracy, we let the political process set restrictions on the use of public property. But there are limits on the exercise of political power. Under our constitutional system, a nonsmoking majority cannot arbitrarily stamp out the rights of a smoking minority. For a regulation to be legitimate, there must be a good fit between the regulation and the goal it seeks to accomplish.

That means smoking should not be banned—even on public property—without showing, first, that the ban will be effective and, second, that it will not proscribe more activities than necessary to reach its objective. Those two showings have not been made. The scientific link between secondhand smoke and various diseases is far from proven—specially on beaches. And regulations often prohibit smoking in locations that are not particularly confining, where patrons can easily avoid harm by taking a step or two away. If the scientific evidence were more compelling and the ban were limited to, say, reading rooms in public libraries, elevators in government office buildings, and restrooms at a state university, then a ban might be warranted. Not otherwise.

Government, not secondhand smoke, is polluting the beaches. Surely we can protect the legitimate rights of non-smokers without prohibiting smokers from relishing an occasional cigarette by the sea.

| "'Just Say No' is a nice slogan, but not a sufficient strategy for protecting our children."

Teens Should Be Taught Responsible Alcohol Use

Tony Newman

In the following viewpoint, Tony Newman argues that his parents did the right thing by allowing him and his friends to drink alcohol at their home while they were teenagers. Newman claims that the "Just Say No" method, or abstinence policy, toward teen drinking and drug use has been ineffective. He concludes that a more realistic approach, which allows for supervised experimentation with alcohol, is a better way to keep teenagers safe. Tony Newman is communications director for the Drug Policy Alliance, an organization that works to establish drug policies.

As you read, consider the following questions:

1. According to the author, why did the author's parents let him and his teenage friends drink alcohol at their house?

2. What percentage of high school seniors will have tried alcohol by the time they graduate, according to the author?

Tony Newman, "'Just Say No' Won't Keep Kids Away from Alcohol," *San Jose Mercury News*, December 3, 2004. www.drugpolicy.org. Reproduced by permission.

3. According to Newman, what goal was more important to his parents than teaching abstinence?

Friday night—four guys, four girls, a case of beer and some wine coolers. My guy friends and I are 17 years old and the girls are 15. We are sitting on couches, listening to Bob Marley and playing the drinking game "quarters."

Allowing Teen Drinking

The goal is to bounce a quarter into a cup. If you make it, you can pick the person who has to drink. If you miss twice in a row, you have to drink. After a few hours of fun and games, the music and the laughter is getting louder and louder. Without warning, the light in the room flicks on and off. All of the laughing stops and there is silence. I tell everyone to chill and walk outside of the shed, across my backyard, up to my parents' bedroom window.

My dad opens the window to his room and tells me, "Keep it down out there."

"OK, Daddy, we will," I assure him.

I return to the shed, smile at my friends and say, "Turn the music down." The guys have been here before and know the routine. One of the girls who is at the shed for the first time can't believe that my parents are just a few feet away in the house.

My parents did know that we—Weasel, Z, Buddo, the new crew of girls that we were starting to hang with, and I—were drinking in the shed. They understood that my friends and I, along with half of my high school classmates, had consumed alcohol and tried marijuana. Although they would have preferred that we didn't drink alcohol or smoke marijuana, they had decided that it was better to have us safe in the backyard where they could keep track of us, instead of having us drive home from a party across town or drink in public.

The Importance of Moderation

The vast majority of teenage drug use (with the exception of nicotine) does not lead to dependence or abusive habits.

Teens who do use alcohol, marijuana and/or other drugs must understand there is a huge difference between use and abuse, and between occasional and daily use.

They should know how to recognize irresponsible behavior when it comes to place, time, dose levels and frequency of use. If young people continue, despite our admonitions, to use alcohol and/or other drugs, they must control their use by practicing moderation and limiting use. It is impossible to do well academically or meet one's responsibilities at work while intoxicated. It is never appropriate to use alcohol and/or other drugs at school, at work, while participating in sports, while driving or engaging in any serious activity.

Marsha Rosenbaum Ph.D.,
Safety First: A Reality-based Approach, *2007.*

During my teenage years in Santa Cruz, Calif. I always appreciated my parents for allowing me and my friends to have a shed in the backyard. Neighborhood kids spent thousands of hours in that shed. We would meet there after surfing. We would meet there before going out on the weekend. We would take our dates there.

Protection over Abstinence

But it is only now, 15 years later, that I understand and respect how brave and protective my parents' actions were. I say brave because my parents were breaking the law and could have been arrested for allowing teenagers to drink at their house. I say protective because they knew that having us in the backyard kept us from the much more risky activity of drinking and driving around town like so many other teens. In addition to allowing us to party in my backyard, my parents made it clear that my friends and I could always call them for a ride home from a party. They preferred a call from a drunk teenager asking for a ride home over a drunk teenager driving his drunk friends all over town.

While most parents hope that their teenagers will not drink alcohol or smoke marijuana, the reality is that 80 percent of high school seniors will have tried alcohol by the time they graduate, and 50 percent will have tried marijuana. "Just Say No" is a nice slogan, but not a sufficient strategy for protecting our children. Despite millions of dollars of scare tactic ads telling kids that smoking pot will fry their brains like an egg, half of 18-year-olds will end up "Just Saying Sometimes" or "Just Saying Yes."

My parents' goal for their two kids was not to practice the unrealistic mission of abstinence, but to keep us safe. In this regard, they were incredibly successful. Their two kids never got into trouble with the law and never got into an accident or a fight that involved alcohol. We learned how to drink in a way that didn't lead to injury to others or to ourselves.

I am at a place in my life where I hope to start a family. I am thankful for the wisdom and example of my parents. I look forward to talking honestly and openly with my children about alcohol and drugs in a way that will, most importantly, keep them as safe as possible.

| *"Underage drinking can no longer be winked at as an inevitable rite of passage."*

The Alcohol Industry Can Help Combat Underage Alcohol Use

Joseph A. Califano, Jr., Julius B. Richmond, Louis W. Sullivan, and David Satcher

In the following viewpoint, Joseph A. Califano, Jr., Julius B. Richmond, Louis W. Sullivan, and David Satcher argue that underage drinking is a serious problem that needs to be addressed. The authors claim that the alcohol industry should help to curb underage and adult excessive drinking. Joseph A. Califano, Jr. was U.S. Secretary of Health, Education and Welfare, and Dr. Julius B. Richmond was U.S. Surgeon General during the Carter administration. Dr. Louis W. Sullivan was U.S. Secretary of Health and Human Services during the George H.W. Bush administration, and Dr. David Satcher was U.S. Surgeon General during the Clinton and George W. Bush administrations.

Joseph A. Califano, Jr., Julius B. Richmond, Louis W. Sullivan, and David Satcher, "The Alcohol Industry's Choice," The National Center on Addiction and Substance Abuse at Columbia University (CASA), February 27, 2003. www.casacolumbia.org. Reproduced by permission.

As you read, consider the following questions:

1. According to research done by the *Journal of the American Medical Association* (*JAMA*), what percentage of beer, wine, and liquor is consumed by children and underage drinkers?
2. What percentage of Americans who drink are underage, according to the authors?
3. According to the authors, what advantages would come from increasing taxes on beer, wine, and liquor?

The study published this week in the *JAMA* (*Journal of the American Medical Association*) which finds that underage drinkers and adult excessive drinking account for half of the alcohol consumed in the U.S. has profound ramifications for public policy, parents and the alcohol industry.

The peer-reviewed analysis reveals that in 1999 (the last year for which necessary data was available) children and underage drinkers consumed 19.7 percent and excessive adult drinking accounted for 30.4 percent of the beer, wine and liquor consumed in the United States. And that estimate of misuse and abuse of alcohol is probably conservative. Researchers used the federal government's health standard for men—in excess of two drinks a day—to calculate the amount of adult excessive drinking for both men and women, when the health standard for women is in excess of one drink a day because of differences in body water and the way in which women metabolize alcohol.

Drinking is a fatal attraction for America's children and underage drinkers. Alcohol is a major contributor to the three leading causes of teen death: accidents, homicide and suicide. Individuals who begin drinking before age 21 are likelier to become adult excessive drinkers. They are more than twice as likely to develop alcohol-related problems. Biomedical research had found that alcohol alters the developing brain and may cause irreversible brain damage.

Moreover, for young Americans there is a correlation between alcohol use and illegal drug use. The Directors of the National Institutes of Drug Abuse and Alcoholism and Alcohol Abuse point out that "12- to 17-year-old youth who consumed alcohol in the past month were 7.6 times more likely to use illicit drugs than those who did not."

Although a recent study by the Harvard School of Public Health suggests that moderate drinking may have some beneficial impact on the heart, there is resounding evidence that excessive drinking is linked to serious health problems such as liver disease, high blood pressure, stroke and many cancers. Alcohol is the number one drug involved in crimes such as rape, assault and murder and in child abuse, domestic violence, family breakup and accidents. In the population 12 and older, heavy binge drinkers (five drinks at one sitting at least five times a month) are eleven times more likely to use illicit drugs like marijuana, cocaine and heroin.

Of Americans who drink, 76 percent are adult moderate drinkers who consume 34 percent of the alcohol. Nine percent are adult excessive drinkers who consume 46.3 percent of the alcohol. The remaining 15 percent are underage drinkers who consume 19.7 percent of the alcohol.

With these revelations about underage and adult excessive drinking, the beer, wine and hard liquor companies face a choice. They must now decide whether they are prepared to cooperate with the public health community to curb such drinking, or whether they intend to walk the walk of the cigarette companies, undermining legislative public health initiatives and fighting lawsuits that claim their marketing activities have encouraged such drinking.

One marker of good faith would be for the alcohol industry to endow a truly independent foundation to mount an aggressive campaign to combat underage and adult excessive drinking. We do not expect an industry that gets half its sales from such drinking to mount a credible campaign against it with institutions like the Century Council, which it controls.

The industry should also voluntarily label its products, detailing all the ingredients and specifying the caloric content. In a survey of girls and young women, the National Center on Addiction and Substance Abuse at Columbia University found that only 56 percent knew alcohol is high in calories and contributes to weight gain. Another 5.7 percent thought that drinking alcohol makes one lose weight (not surprisingly, these young women drank more than the others). Every beer container and bottle of wine and hard liquor should bear a label warning against underage and excessive adult drinking and listing the consumption standards established by the U.S. Departments of Health and Human Services and Agriculture— e.g., "More than two drinks a day for men and more than one drink a day for women is hazardous to your health."

Federal, state and local governments can promote the public health and ease their budgetary problems by increasing taxes on beer, wine and liquor. Increasing the cost of alcoholic beverages offers a triple win to hard pressed governments: it will discourage underage and adult excessive drinking and decrease the related health care and criminal justice costs, it will lower their deficits, and it will reduce illegal drug use.

Alcohol is the number one drug of abuse for young Americans. Revealing the widespread extent of underage drinking and the often related adult excessive drinking triggers a loud alarm for parents and schools: Underage drinking can no longer be winked at as an inevitable rite of passage; it must be recognized as the grim game of Russian roulette it is, a game far too dangerous to ignore or accept among our youngsters.

Periodical Bibliography

The following articles have been selected to supplement the diverse views presented in this chapter.

Paul Armentano "Testing Students for Drugs Is Neither Solution nor Bargain," *Fort Wayne (IN) New Sentinel*, September 21, 2005.

Arthur Bosse "Designing Effective Youth Prevention Programming," *Addiction Professional*, March 2005.

Burlington Free Press "Lowering Drinking Age No Solution to Abuse," February 27, 2007.

Brian S. Flynn et al. "Mass Media and Community Interventions to Reduce Alcohol Use by Early Adolescents," *Journal of Studies on Alcohol*, January 2006.

Thomas A. Lambert "The Case against Smoking Bans," *Regulation*, Winter 2006–2007.

Jay Matthews "Why You Shouldn't Teach Moderate Drinking," *Washington Post*, May 4, 2004.

Bill McKelway "How Kids Can Drink at Home, Legally," *Richmond Times-Dispatch*, January 28, 2007.

Marsha Rosenbaum "DARE: The Never-Ending Folly," *Orange County Register*, April 14, 2005.

Debra J. Saunders "The Failed War on Pot Users," *San Francisco Chronicle*, October 20, 2005.

Eric Schlosser "Make Peace with Pot," *The New York Times*, April 26, 2004.

Curren Warf and Alain Joffe "Response to the American Academy of Pediatrics Report on Legalization of Marijuana," *Pediatrics*, November 2005.

Ray Warren "Because Marijuana Eradication Policy Is Hopeless, Tax and Regulate Instead," *Los Angeles Daily Journal*, July 19, 2007.

For Further Discussion

Chapter 1

1. In David J. Hanson's interview with Andrew L. Golub, Golub distinguishes between the stepping stone theory of drug use and the gateway theory of drug use. Jacob Sullum argues that the popularity of the gateway theory is partly due to the ambiguity of what it means. Considering Sullum's claim about the ambiguity of the theory, which of Golub's theories do you think people have in mind when they call for more restrictive policies toward gateway drugs? Do you think that Golub's distinction matters when thinking about policies toward drugs?

2. Kimberly R. Martin reports on research in favor of the gateway effect of alcohol, tobacco, and marijuana. Central to the theory of the gateway effect of alcohol, tobacco, and marijuana is the idea that use of these drugs creates "drug exposure opportunities," with users of the gateway substances more likely to take these opportunities. According to the research by Andrew R. Morral, how does the common-factor model account for the correlation between use of marijuana and other illicit drugs without relying on the existence of a drug exposure opportunity as a determinant cause of use?

3. Stephen Pudney argues that it is personal characteristics, and not a gateway effect, that cause people to use drugs of all kinds. If this is true, how might the evidence appear consistent with the hypothesis of a gateway effect? What kind of evidence would you look for to resolve the debate?

Chapter 2

1. The Office of National Drug Control Policy claims that marijuana is harmful and addictive, whereas Paul Armentano attempts to refute these claims. After reading both, whom do you agree with more regarding a) the harmfulness and b) the addictiveness of marijuana? Use specific textual examples to back up your answers.

2. Albert S. Whiting argues that no amount of alcohol is safe and the National Institute of Drug Abuse (NIDA) viewpoint implies that no amount of tobacco is safe or desirable. David J. Hanson and Joe Jackson offer contrasting views on alcohol and tobacco, respectively: Hanson claims that the harms of alcohol are overstated and that a certain amount of alcohol is not harmful but is actually beneficial; Jackson claims that the harms of tobacco are overstated, and that moderate smoking is not harmful and may also be beneficial. What information within the contrasting views on alcohol and tobacco use is most compelling to you in deciding whether to use these drugs? Explain, citing specific material from the four viewpoints.

Chapter 3

1. The National Center on Addiction and Substance Abuse at Columbia University (CASA); Patrick Zickler; Alyssa J. Myers and Marion O. Petty; and J. C. Gfroerer, Li-Tzy Wu, and M. A. Penne all make claims about the gateway effect of a particular drug. Among the four, distinguish the specific evidence each party uses to back up its claims of a gateway effect; how is this evidence different and how is it similar?

2. Bruce Mirken claims that it is marijuana's classification as an illegal drug that creates a gateway to other illegal drugs like cocaine and speed (methamphetamine). If this is true, what kinds of statistical changes in drug use would one expect to see if marijuana was legalized? What

would Mirken say to Gfroerer, Wu, and Penne about the conclusions they draw from the data of their study?

Chapter 4

1. Ray Warren argues that marijuana is not dangerous and should be legalized, whereas Antonio Maria Costa argues that marijuana is dangerous and should not be legalized. Rosie Boycott agrees in part with both of them. Identify the specific areas of agreement and disagreement between both Boycott and Warren, and Boycott and Costa.

2. John W. Whitehead points to the dangers of smoking to support his view that tobacco use should be outlawed. Robert A. Levy does not consider the dangers of smoking to the smokers themselves, instead emphasizing the importance of smokers' rights to smoke. How do you think society's interest in protecting people from harm ought to be balanced with respect for individual rights?

3. Tony Newman does not believe that teaching young people to abstain from alcohol is realistic given the fact that a high percentage of young people try alcohol by the time they graduate from high school. Joseph A. Califano, Jr., Julius B. Richmond, Louis W. Sullivan, and David Satcher take a different approach, arguing that the alcohol industry needs to do more to prevent underage drinking. Do you think that the issue of underage drinking ought to be addressed by parents allowing alcohol use at home, further action by the alcohol industry, or in some other way? Explain your answer.

Organizations to Contact

The editors have compiled the following list of organizations concerned with the issues debated in this book. The descriptions are derived from materials provided by the organizations. All have publications or information available for interested readers. The list was compiled on the date of publication of the present volume; the information provided here may change. Readers need to remember that many organizations take several weeks or longer to respond to inquiries.

American Civil Liberties Union (ACLU)
125 Broad St., 18th Floor, New York, NY   10004
(212) 549-2500
e-mail: aclu@aclu.org
Web site: www.aclu.org

The ACLU is a national organization that works to defend Americans' civil rights guaranteed by the U.S. Constitution by providing legal defense, research, and education. The ACLU opposes the criminal prohibition of marijuana and the civil liberties violations that result from it. Its publications include *Making Sense of Student Drug Testing: Why Educators Are Saying No.*

American Council for Drug Education (ACDE)
164 W. Seventy-fourth St., New York, NY   10023
(800) 488-3784 • fax: (212) 595-2553
e-mail: acde@phoenixhouse.org
Web site: www.acde.org

The American Council for Drug Education seeks to diminish substance abuse. It creates accessible materials on the most current scientific research to those seeking accurate, compelling information on drugs. ACDE has resources about drug and alcohol abuse for parents, youth, educators, prevention professionals, employers, health care professionals, and other concerned community members, including fact sheets on numerous substances. ACDE is an affiliate of Phoenix House Foundation, the largest, private, nonprofit drug abuse service agency in the country.

The American Legacy Foundation
2030 M St., NW, 6th Floor, Washington, DC   20036
(202) 454-5555 • fax: (202) 454-5999
e-mail: info@americanlegacy.org
Web site: www.americanlegacy.org

The American Legacy Foundation is dedicated to building a world where young people reject tobacco and anyone can quit using tobacco. The foundation works on the national tobacco youth prevention and education campaign, the *Truth* campaign. It conducts extensive research on tobacco-related issues and publishes the results in their *First Look Reports*, a series of brief summaries of their research.

Cato Institute
1000 Massachusetts Ave., NW, Washington, DC   20001-5403
(202) 842-0200 • fax: (202) 842-3490
e-mail: cato@cato.org
Web site: www.cato.org

The institute is a public policy research foundation dedicated to limiting the control of government and to protecting individual liberty. The Cato Institute strongly favors drug legalization. The institute publishes the *Cato Journal* three times a year and the *Cato Policy Report* bimonthly.

Choose Responsibility
PO Box 507, Middlebury, VT   05753
(802) 398-2024
e-mail: info@chooseresponsibility.org
Web site: www.chooseresponsibility.org

Choose Responsibility works to engage young people, their parents, and public officials in serious deliberation on the role of alcohol in American culture. The organization advocates a multi-faceted approach that combines education, certification, and provisional licensing for 18- to 20-year-old high school graduates who choose to consume alcohol. The Web site contains facts about underage drinking and a model alcohol education curriculum.

Drug Policy Alliance

70 W. Thirty-sixth St., 16th Floor, New York, NY   10018
(212) 613-8020 • fax: (212) 613-8021
e-mail: nyc@drugpolicy.org
Web site: www.drugpolicy.org

The Drug Policy Alliance, an independent nonprofit organization created in 2000 when the Lindesmith Center merged with the Drug Policy Foundation, supports and publicizes alternatives to current U.S. policies on illegal drugs, including marijuana. The alliance sponsors Safety First, a drug education program that advocates the harm-reduction approach to curbing teen drug use. Their Web site contains recent news on drug policy and links to other resources. Among the alliance's recent publications is the booklet for parents, *Safety First: A Reality-Based Approach to Teens and Drugs.*

Join Together

715 Albany St., 580-3rd Floor, Boston, MA   02118
(617) 437-1500 • fax: (617) 437-9394
e-mail: info@jointogether.org
Web site: www.jointogether.org

Founded in 1991, Join Together supports community-based efforts to advance effective alcohol and drug policy, prevention, and treatment. It leads initiatives to help communities respond to the harms caused by excessive alcohol and drug use and provides free internet services supporting their efforts. Among its publications is the guide for community leaders, *Ten Drug and Alcohol Policies That Will Save Lives.*

Marijuana Policy Project

PO Box 77492, Capitol Hill, Washington, DC   20013
(202) 462-5747
e-mail: mpp@mpp.org
Web site: www.mpp.org

The Marijuana Policy Project works to further public policies that allow for responsible medical and nonmedical use of marijuana and that minimize the harms associated with marijuana consumption and the laws that manage its use. It works to increase public support for marijuana regulation and lobbies for marijuana policy reform at the state and federal levels. The project increases public awareness through speaking engagements, educational seminars, the mass media, and briefing papers.

The National Center on Addiction and Substance Abuse (CASA) at Columbia University

633 Third Ave., 19th Floor, New York, NY   10017-6706
(212) 841-5200
Web site: www.casacolumbia.org

CASA is a private nonprofit organization that aims to inform Americans of the economic and social costs of substance abuse and its impact on their lives, while also removing the stigma of substance abuse and replacing shame and despair with hope. The organization supports treatment as the best way to reduce chemical dependency. CASA publishes numerous reports and books, including *Women Under the Influence*.

The National Council on Alcoholism and Drug Dependence (NCADD)

244 East Fifty-eighth Street, 4th Floor, New York, NY   10022
(212) 269-7797
e-mail: national@ncadd.org
Web site: www.ncadd.org

The NCADD works to fight the stigma and the disease of alcoholism and other drug addictions. It publishes numerous pamphlets including *What Are the Signs of Alcoholism?* and

Drinking Too Much Too Fast Can Kill You. In addition, it publishes the *Washington Report,* a monthly Washington, D.C.-based public policy newsletter, and *NCADD Amethyst,* a quarterly informational newsletter covering major issues in the field.

National Institute on Alcohol Abuse and Alcoholism (NIAAA)
5635 Fishers Lane, MSC 9304, Bethesda, MD   20892-9304
(301) 443-3860
Web site: www.niaaa.nih.gov

The NIAAA aims to reduce alcohol-related problems through conducting research and disseminating research findings to health care providers, researchers, policy makers and the public. It publishes the quarterly bulletin *Alcohol Alert* for researchers and health professionals. For the general public, it publishes pamphlets, brochures, fact sheets, and the newsletter *Frontlines.*

National Institute on Drug Abuse (NIDA)
6001 Executive Blvd., Rm. 5213 MSC 9561
Bethesda, MD   20892-9561
(301) 443-6245
e-mail: information@nida.nih.gov
Web site: www.nida.nih.gov

NIDA supports and conducts research on drug abuse—including the yearly *Monitoring the Future Survey*—to improve addiction prevention, treatment, and policy efforts. It publishes the bimonthly *NIDA Notes* newsletter, the periodic *NIDA Capsules* fact sheets, and a catalog of research reports and public education materials, such as *Marijuana: Facts for Teens* and *Marijuana: Facts Parents Need to Know.*

National Organization for the Reform of Marijuana Laws (NORML)
1600 K St., NW, Suite 501, Washington, DC   20006-2832
(202) 483-5500 • fax: (202) 483-0057

e-mail: norml@norml.org
website: www.norml.org

NORML's mission is to move public opinion to achieve the repeal of marijuana prohibition so that the responsible use of cannabis by adults is no longer subject to penalty. NORML serves as an informational resource on marijuana-related stories, and lobbies state and federal legislators in support of reform legislation. NORML has numerous research and position papers available at their Web site, including *Rethinking the Consequences of Decriminalizing Marijuana.*

New York Coalition of Social Smokers
PO Box 704, Commack, NY   11725
e-mail: info@socialsmokers.org
Web site: www.socialsmokers.org

The New York Coalition of Social Smokers works to protect the rights of smokers and non-smokers. Their goal is to preserve the rights of smokers by working to limit smoking bans that severely curtail the ability to smoke. The coalition publishes *The United Pro Choice Smokers Rights Newletter* weekly, which is available at their Web site.

Office of National Drug Control Policy (ONDCP)
Drug Policy Information Clearinghouse, PO Box 6000
Rockville, MD   20849-6000
(800) 666-3332 • fax: (301) 519-5212
e-mail: ondcp@ncjrs.org
website: www.whitehousedrugpolicy.gov

The Office of National Drug Control Policy, a component of the Executive Office of the President, establishes policies, priorities, and objectives for the Nation's drug control program. The ONDCP works to reduce illicit drug use, manufacturing, and trafficking; drug-related crime and violence; and drug-related health consequences. The ONDCP has numerous publications related to its mission, including *Marijuana Myths & Facts: The Truth Behind 10 Popular Misperceptions.*

Bibliography of Books

Nikki Babbit   *Adolescent Drug and Alcohol Abuse: How to Spot It, Stop It, and Get Help for Your Family.* Sebastapol, CA: O'Reilly, 2000.

Arthur W. Blume   *Treating Drug Problems.* Hoboken, NJ: Wiley, 2005.

Alan Bock   *Waiting to Inhale: The Politics of Medical Marijuana.* Santa Ana, CA: Seven Locks Press, 2000.

Allan M. Brandt   *The Cigarette Century: The Rise, Fall, and Deadly Persistence of the Product That Defined America.* New York: Basic Books, 2007.

Eric Burns   *The Smoke of the Gods: A Social History of Tobacco.* Philadelphia, PA: Temple University Press, 2007.

Rosalyn Carson-DeWitt, ed.   *Drugs, Alcohol, and Tobacco: Learning About Addictive Behavior.* New York: Macmillan Reference USA, 2003.

Jonathan P. Caulkins et al.   *School-Based Drug Prevention: What Kind of Drug Use Does it Prevent?* Santa Monica, CA: Rand, 2002.

Mitch Earleywine   *Understanding Marijuana: A New Look at the Scientific Evidence.* New York: Oxford University Press, 2002.

Griffith Edwards   *Matters of Substance: Drugs—and Why Everyone's a User.* New York: Thomas Dunne, 2004.

Richard Fields

Drugs in Perspective: A Personalized Look at Substance Use and Abuse. New York: McGraw-Hill, 2004.

Paul Gahlinger

Illegal Drugs. New York: Penguin, 2003.

Victoria C. G. Greenleaf.

Fighting the Good Fight: One Family's Struggle against Adolescent Alcoholism. Fort Bragg, CA: Cypress House, 2002.

Ralph Harris and Judith Hatton

Murder a Cigarette: The Smoking Debate. London: Duckworth, 1998.

Margaret O. Hyde and John F. Setaro

Smoking 101: An Overview for Teens. Minneapolis, MN: Twenty-First Century Books, 2006.

Institute of Medicine

Reducing Underage Drinking: A Collective Responsibility. Washington, DC: National Academies Press, 2004.

Denise B. Kandel, ed.

Stages and Pathways of Drug Involvement: Examining the Gateway Hypothesis. New York: Cambridge University Press, 2002.

Katherine Ketcham

Teens Under the Influence: The Truth about Kids, Alcohol, and Other Drugs—How to Recognize the Problem and What to Do about It. New York: Ballantine Books, 2003.

Cynthia Kuhn et al.

Buzzed: The Straight Facts about the Most Used and Abused Drugs from Alcohol to Ecstasy. New York: W. W. Norton & Company, 2003.

Bill Manville — *Cool, Hip, and Sober: 88 Ways to Beat Booze and Drugs.* New York: Tom Doherty Associates, 2003.

Shelly Marshall — *Young, Sober, and Free: Experience, Strength, and Hope for Young Adults.* Center City, MN: Hazelden, 2003.

Marilyn McClellan — *The Big Deal about Alcohol: What Teens Need to Know about Drinking.* Berkeley Heights, NJ: Enslow Publishers, 2004.

Michael Rabinoff — *Ending the Tobacco Holocaust.* Santa Rosa, CA: Elite Books, 2006.

Joyce Brennfleck Shannon, ed. — *Alcohol Information for Teens: Health Tips about Alcohol and Alcoholism.* Detroit, MI: Omnigraphics, 2004.

Sally J. Stevens and Andrew R. Morral — *Adolescent Substance Abuse Treatment in the United States: Exemplary Models from a National Evaluation Study.* Binghamton, NY: Haworth, 2003.

Andrew T. Weil and Winifred Rosen — *From Chocolate to Morphine: Everything You Need to Know about Mind-Altering Drugs.* New York: Houghton Mifflin, 2004.

Bettie B. Youngs, Jennifer Leigh Youngs, and Tina Moreno — *A Teen's Guide to Living Drug Free.* Deerfield Beach, FL: Health Communications, 2003.

Koren Zailckas — *Smashed: Story of a Drunken Girlhood.* New York: Penguin, 2005.

Index

A

Abstinence
  alcohol-related deaths and, 90
  vs. protection, 172–173
Acetaldehyde, 97–98, 101
Addiction
  to marijuana, 59, 61–63,
    74–75
  to tobacco, 95–98, 109–111,
    163
  treatment for, 123–124
Adolescents. *See* Teenagers
Adrenaline, 95
Adverse effects
  of alcohol, 78–84, 176
  of marijuana, 57–66, 153–155,
    157–158
  of smoking during pregnancy,
    100
  of tobacco, 93–94, 98–99,
    103–108, 162–163
Advertising, alcohol, 89–90, 126
Aggressive behavior
  alcohol use and, 76–77
  marijuana use and, 64, 76–77
  skunk and, 155
Alcohol
  absorption of, 79, 87
  availability of, 14, 126
  cognitive functioning and, 89
  effects of, on body, 80–83
  as gateway drug, 30–31
  impact of, on youth, 81
  regulation of, 144
  risk-taking behavior and,
    76–77
  as soft drug, 55
Alcohol advertising, 89–90, 126

Alcohol industry, underage drinking and, 174–177
Alcohol tolerance, 83–84, 90
Alcohol use
  among college students, 91
  criminal behavior and, 127,
    176
  cultural theory of, 26
  as gateway to marijuana use,
    125–131
  harmful effects of, 78–84, 176
  moderation in, 172
  myths of harms of, 85–91
  statistics on, 15, 126, 176
  underage, 81, 88–89, 170–177
  in U.S., 89
Alcoholics Anonymous (AA), 91
Alcoholism, 87, 90–91
Allison, Graham, 25
Amondson, Gene, 145
Anderson, R. Warren, 115
Anslinger, Harry, 48
Anthony, James C., 30–33
Anxiety, 59
Armentano, Paul, 67
Asthma, 98–99
Automobile accidents
  alcohol-related, 81
  marijuana use and, 60, 72–74,
    158

B

"Beer belly," 86
Binge drinking, 87–88, 127
Birth weights, smoking and, 100
Blaze-Temple, Debra, 126–127